# SCREENWRITING FOR MICRO-BUDGET FILMS

Screenwriting for micro-budget films can present its own challenges and this book takes the reader through all the considerations that need to be made to write an effective screenplay for a low-budget film.

Drawing on his own experience, case studies from films such as Primer, Coherence and Reservoir Dogs, as well as the perspectives of working screenwriters such as Joe Swanberg and Alex Ross-Perry, Greenberg explores common pitfalls screenwriters face and suggests practical solutions. This book lays the groundworks of the realities of low-budget filmmaking and also talks through the practical aspects, such as story structure and genre considerations. Greenberg makes the process of writing a screenplay for a low-budget film accessible and creative, allowing student and independent filmmakers to tailor their writing for their films.

This book is ideal for aspiring screenwriters, independent filmmakers and students of screenwriting.

**David J. Greenberg** teaches screenwriting at Drexel University and the University of the Arts in Philadelphia. He has written nearly 60 screenplays for features, documentaries and shorts. He wrote and directed the feature Stomping Ground (2016) which was produced for $18,000 and shot in 24 hours.

# SCREENWRITING FOR MICRO-BUDGET FILMS

Tips, Tricks and Hacks for Reverse Engineering Your Screenplay

*David J. Greenberg*

Routledge
Taylor & Francis Group

LONDON AND NEW YORK

First published 2022
by Routledge
2 Park Square, Milton Park, Abingdon, Oxon OX14 4RN

and by Routledge
605 Third Avenue, New York, NY 10158

*Routledge is an imprint of the Taylor & Francis Group, an informa business*

*British Library Cataloguing-in-Publication Data*
A catalogue record for this book is available from the British Library

*Library of Congress Cataloging-in-Publication Data*
Names: Greenberg, David J., author.
Title: Screenwriting for micro-budget films / David J. Greenberg.
Description: Abingdon, Oxon ; New York, NY : Routledge, 2022. | Includes bibliographical references and index.
Identifiers: LCCN 2021031300 (print) | LCCN 2021031301 (ebook) | ISBN 9780367687700 (hardback) | ISBN 9780367687694 (paperback) | ISBN 9781003138969 (ebook)
Subjects: LCSH: Low budget films—Authorship. | Independent films—Authorship. | Motion picture authorship—Vocational guidance.
Classification: LCC PN1996.G74 2022 (print) | LCC PN1996 (ebook) | DDC 808.2/3—dc23
LC record available at https://lccn.loc.gov/2021031300
LC ebook record available at https://lccn.loc.gov/2021031301

ISBN: 978-0-367-68770-0 (hbk)
ISBN: 978-0-367-68769-4 (pbk)
ISBN: 978-1-003-13896-9 (ebk)

DOI: 10.4324/9781003138969

Typeset in Bembo
by Apex CoVantage, LLC

# CONTENTS

# INTRODUCTION

A funny thing happened to me while I was writing this book. I was teaching my screenwriting classes, working on three screenplays for hire and a documentary when a filmmaker friend called. He asked if I had time to read a screenplay he was thinking about directing. I read it, a sharp, witty horror-comedy and, at 77 pages, only two or three locations, around eight characters, no big set pieces or special effects, it was a great example of a screenplay that could be well produced on a micro-budget. I called my friend immediately after reading it and said "You have to make this film and I will do whatever I can to help." He said "Great, what do you want to do?" That was not the response I was expecting, but it would have looked bad to contradict myself, so the next thing out of my mouth was "Umm, produce?"

While, technically, I had done some producing on my feature Stomping Ground (2016), it was not a role I felt comfortable in, ever sought out and, to be completely honest, it was something I actively avoided. But, I felt strongly that this film deserved to be produced and I committed to it. The first and the best thing I did as a producer was ask if I could show it to my friend Andy Silverman, a screenwriter who had recently started producing, notably his amazing horror-comedy Cyst, which has "midnight movie" and "cult film" written all over it. We had been meeting weekly at a bakery down the street from me, I told him about the screenplay, and he read it and signed

DOI: 10.4324/9781003138969-1

on as a producer. That's it; I just thought it was worth mentioning that, as I write this book, I am also producing a micro-budget film. What does producing a micro-budget film mean? It probably means different things to different people. In my case, producing means everything from cleaning toilets, washing dishes and loading/unloading equipment to scouting locations, hiring personnel and playing a homeless person.

In the end, we decided that producing a film with eight characters and a crew of ten would be too tricky to do safely in early 2021, with the COVID-19 pandemic still raging on. We turned our attention to another screenplay by the same writer. It was 99% two characters in one location. In May and June of 2021, we went to the Pocono Mountains for nine days and lived in the huge house where we were shooting and we produced Seclusion, which I will discuss in greater detail in the chapter on writing for producers.

Next, I want to point out that the name of this book is "Screenwriting For Micro Budget Films," not "How To Write Micro Budget Films." Of course, the book is about how to write a screenplay for a micro-budget film, but, in my experience, there is no "one" way to it. With that in mind, I present various approaches to it from my own philosophy but also include interviews with filmmakers whose background, philosophy and approach differ from or even contradict mine. I have found that, if you disagree with someone's way of thinking, it usually forces you to refine, clarify and solidify your own. I do not necessarily want you to come away from reading this book thinking that you should follow one of the models described, I want you to come away from reading this book having heard about the different ways to write a micro-budget film and then use the ones that you agree with to come up with your own way of writing a screenplay.

To backtrack a little and fill in some blanks, I want to get into my lifelong love affair with film. One of my earliest memories is of toddling down the street, one hand in each of my parent's hands, and going to a repertory movie house in Philadelphia. I am pretty sure that this was the day that I saw a film in a theater for the first time. I think it was Charlie Chaplin's The Gold Rush (1925). In first grade, we had a classroom guest who brought in a video camera. Keep in mind that, in 1971, few people were walking around with video cameras. I can still remember looking through the viewfinder and, at six years old, thinking "I like this!"

My mom had worked as an actress in her teens and through college. My father had been a professional tap dancer, appearing on a weekly TV show in Philadelphia and did summer stock (four musicals per summer) in Atlantic City. Both were writers and English teachers, so I grew up with an appreciation for the arts. If hippies deigned to carry cards, my parents would have been card-carrying hippies. I like to say that I was raised on classic rock and soul, classical music and show tunes. My father liked to show movies in class and this period was before we had video stores so, in order to get movies, he could rent them from a distributor or borrow them from the Free Library of Philadelphia, which printed a huge catalog of their holdings. I can remember reading through that catalog at six or seven, reading the synopsis of films and trying to imagine them in my mind.

I made my first (animated) films when I was nine, bought a super 8 camera when I was ten and made films with friends. Around that time, I saw Jaws (1975) and North By Northwest on the big screen, something clicked and I just said something like "this is what I want to do" to myself.

When I was 16, I found out about film school. Do you mean, you can go to college and study movies? I did go to film school and I guess I am pretty glad that I did though I am not exactly sure what I got out of it. For someone who loves film, it was total immersion, I learned theory/esthetics, history, production, etc., and I loved it.

The first time I was really conscious of saying the words "independent film" as in "I'm going to an independent film tonight" was when I went to see the Coen Brothers debut Blood Simple (1984)— itself a masterpiece overall but also a prime example of high-end low-budget filmmaking, and a production model followed by scores of would-be indie filmmakers ever since. I know that I had seen low-budget independent films before, but this time it felt different. I guess I was a sophomore in film school when Blood Simple came out so, by the time I graduated in 1987, I had become well aware of not just the Coens but Jim Jarmusch, Spike Lee, Susan Seidelman and so many more. Not long after graduation, I went out to lunch with my dad, who asked if I was going to move to L.A. and I said "No, there's all of these people coming out of 'nowhere' making films for nothing with friends and family in their backyards and that's what I want to do."

I didn't make my own friends and family film in the backyard until 2013. More on that story later.

So I did not move to L.A. after graduation in 1987 and I did not start making my own low-budget independent film; I did about as opposite as possible from filmmaking and got just about as far away from L.A. in the geographical United States as possible. My father was closing his bakery-cafe in Frenchtown, NJ, and reopening it in Blue Hill, ME. Since I was literally doing nothing, not working and nowhere close to having a "real" job, it was gently or perhaps not so gently suggested that I move up to Maine with my dad and help renovate the building. It was around this time that I started writing my first feature-length screenplay, a run-of-the-mill, by-the-books teen thriller called Play With Fire. Okay, technically, it was not my first feature-length screenplay because I had written Pinball, a sort of junior high spin on Saturday Night Fever (1977) in longhand when I was 13. I stayed in Blue Hill until the December of 1987, moved back to Philly and did what any film school graduate not working in the film business would do. I got a job in a video store, in this case, Philadelphia's Mecca for filmlovers, TLA Video.

I didn't last in Philly long because, the following spring, my father told me that, of all things, a low-budget independent film was going to be shooting in Blue Hill. Some of the advance team was already in town, coming to my dad's place, The Left Bank, regularly. He told them about his son who just got out of film school and got a contact number for me. I called the Unit Production Manager every week for about a month but he wouldn't commit to giving me a job, so, one day, I just flew up to Maine, walked into the production office, introduced myself and he said "Oh, you're here." I told him about everything I studied in film school, he nodded politely, then pointed to a bunch of guys raising a huge tent outside and said "See those guys? Go help them." We got the tent up, came back in, the UPM asked one of the other guys how I did, got a nod from him, turned to me and said "You're hired and it doesn't pay." The UPM was Daniel Lupi. It was his second feature. Before movies, I think he managed a restaurant in Manhattan. If you can manage a restaurant in Manhattan, you can produce a movie. Today, Daniel has executive produced Us, Her, all of Paul Thomas Anderson's films, a few for Spielberg and many others.

On the relatively low-budget Signs of Life (1989), I wound up working as a P.A. wherever I was needed, in every department. One day, things were sort of slow, so Daniel told me to get the producer's car washed. When I got back, he asked "what do you know about cameras?" It was just a year after film school and, while I was never an especially good director of photography (DP), there was a time when I could load an old Bolex without looking at it. Anyway, the First AC had to leave the set because he was sick, the Second AC took his job and, all of a sudden, I was the Second AC for the day. It was not until I later offered to take the place of the set security guard who quit his all-night position that I started getting paid $50 a day. I once worked all day, all night and then the next day, something like 45 hours straight on set.

Two days after Signs of Life wrapped, I started work on the considerably higher-budget Pet Sematary (1989). In stark contrast to the Signs of Life shoot, I had one job in one department, regular hours and, for a fairly recent film school graduate, I was making pretty decent money—as the set-construction department runner. The what? I drove around and bought building supplies all day and then delivered them either to the workshop or right to set. How low on the ladder is this position? It's not even on the ladder. My name is not even in the credits of the film. On one set, I could see people pitching in to help each other, a small community with limited resources striving toward the same goal. On another set, I saw bureaucracy, rivalries, petty arguments between departments and a sort of all-for-one-none-for-all kind of attitude. It was a life-changing experience and drew me even closer toward the direction of smaller, independent films. I told myself then that, if I ever got a chance to make a film, it would be a financially responsible production.

At the end of being on sets for nearly nine months straight, I had a revelation that I could probably continue to do this kind of work for the next 40 years of my life, but that it was not what I really wanted to do. At that point, I had worked in almost every department of a film production and, while, of course, every shoot is different, there was an overwhelming sense that I would be basically doing the same thing over and over again for the rest of my professional life.

Also, at this point, the role of the screenwriter was becoming more clear to me. I saw Woody Allen's Crimes and Misdemeanors (1989) around this time and loved it. Something that stood out to me was that Allen's character was a documentary filmmaker working on a project about a philosopher. There were scenes of footage he was editing, and after hearing a few lines from the philosopher character, I thought to myself "Well, that's an interesting philosophy, I need to look into this guy. Funny that I have never heard of him." Funny that I had never heard of him? He was a fictional character and the philosophy he was spouting was movie dialogue written by Woody Allen. Suddenly, at that point, I said to myself "Woah, that's what a screenwriter does?"

I decided that screenwriting was my way in; it is what I do best and enjoy most so that is where my attention shifted.

I had always been a decent creative writer, encouraged to write from a pretty young age, but never really focused on it in film school. I wanted to be a writer-director, figured I sort of had the writing part down, so I set about learning as much of the production side as I could. Turns out, in addition to not being a great cinematographer, I am even worse as an editor. One professor literally ripped a film of mine to shreds. In the spirit of full disclosure, now is as good a time as any to reveal that I got a B− in screenwriting class. On the other hand, I wrote and shot an original scene for a project in directing class and the professor said "Good scene. Is that Mamet?" So, if nothing else was remarkable about my film school career, a professor did think that my original work might have been something by David Mamet.

So, after Signs of Life and Pet Sematary in 1988, other than a few shorts and a pilot I was hired to direct, I did not work on another feature film set until I made Stomping Ground in 2013 and Seclusion in 2021. I focused on writing screenplays and studying the ins and outs of the industry. I wrote low-budget indie type stuff that everyone was doing in the early 1990s, stuff that I could produce myself if I could raise the $30–50,000 (which I could not). Between 1991 and 1994, I eventually made The True Meaning of Cool (1995), which I had written in 1989, basically a shorter version (although there is a feature-length version of it somewhere) of Richard Linklater's Slacker (1990), which won an award from the American Film Institute. Pretty impressive, AFI, right? No, not really, it was a runner-up award from Sony's Visions of U.S. short film competition, which was sponsored by the AFI. Hey, it was still the AFI, the trophy says "American Film Institute" on it, so I can call myself an AFI award-winning filmmaker and that phrase has been opening doors for years.

Through a contact at a record company, I got a couple of low-rent screenwriting jobs in the mid-90s, adapting some true crime books into ideas for films that could feature soundtracks by the record company's artists. I did not get another screenwriting gig until 2007—true story: my then-wife decided to do CPR on my career by employing feng-shui. She rearranged the "career" section of our house and put a couple of my screenplays on a desk by the front door. I got hired to write a screenplay two weeks later and, two weeks after that, got hired to write another screenplay.

To me, screenwriting is almost a spiritual quest, a never-ending journey to learn more about the craft, art and science. I love that, every time I sit down to work on a screenplay, it is going to be a new experience; it is about knowing what tools I have access to and then figuring out the best way to use them. The day I tell myself that I am a good screenwriter, is the day I should quit.

The purpose of this book is to guide filmmakers toward making the best films with limited resources by starting in the conceptual phase, writing the screenplay. While the principles of dramatic storytelling are basically the same as they are for films produced with seemingly endless pots of gold, writing for low-budget films requires a much different technical and creative approach that many screenwriters are not familiar with. My intent for this book is to not only lay out the savvy and successful way to approach a project that is likely to be produced for little money, but it will also have case studies examining the ways notable low-budget productions had cost-saving techniques built in from the beginning, in the screenplay.

In 1991, Francis Ford Coppola famously suggested that "To me, the great hope is that now these little 8mm video recorders and stuff have come out, and some . . . just people who normally wouldn't make movies are going to be making them. And you know, suddenly, one day some little fat girl in Ohio is going to be the new Mozart, you know, and make a beautiful film with her little father's camera recorder. And for once, the so-called professionalism about movies will be destroyed, forever. And it will really become an art form. That's my opinion" and if it has not exactly turned out that way, it is awfully close to being accurate.

With the rapid development of digital production tools over the past 30 years, filmmaking is something that anyone equipped with a smartphone can pursue. Of course, just as in the case of major Hollywood productions with budgets in the hundreds of millions of dollars, technology means little if the filmmaker does not have a good story to tell. In the case of low-budget films, there are certain hacks to learn and many pitfalls to avoid before showing up on set; these things need to be integral to the foundation of the production, key components of the screenplay.

So, today, more than 30 years after Copolla's proclamation, if it seems like everyone's grandmother or a next-door neighbor is an "independent filmmaker," it is because many grandmothers and people in our neighborhoods are making films. I know grandmothers and neighbors of mine who are making films.

Low-budget films have been around forever. In the earliest days of filmmaking in the United States, Thomas Edison held the patents for film, cameras and projectors. A filmmaker could not make a film without paying Edison, but many still tried. Edison reportedly employed armed gangs to track down independent filmmakers who tried to make underground—what many of us now call "guerrilla"—productions without paying him. While Edison's monopoly was ultimately broken up, filmmakers working outside of the established system have always had problems finding ways to make their movies. Over the years, filmmakers have found more and more hacks for making films with less and less resources. This book is about the hacks that writers can build into a screenplay.

Back to film history but skipping ahead to the Golden Age of Hollywood, roughly the 1930s to the 1950s, B-movies, low-budget productions often just over an hour-long, accompanied prestige A-movies, the higher budget films with big-name actors, as a sort of two-for-one deal. When we think of B-movies, many of us think of gritty crime thrillers or frequently cheesy horror movies. On the one hand, we often think of shadowy film noir movies with their bleak themes, relatively small-scale stories and, yes, shadowy imagery highly influenced by German Expressionism. All of these characteristics are evident, but what might not have been so obvious was that, according to many, these films were so dark and shadowy because the budgets were too small to utilize a full arsenal of major studio lights. Directors, cinematographers, grips and gaffers had to get creative with their lighting, creating mood and atmosphere with shadows when lavish sets were not at their disposal. In other words, they used financial limitations to their advantage, taking what might have been a challenging disadvantage to some filmmakers and turning creative workarounds into artistic wins. Contrast the stylish film noir canon with the low-budget monster and science fiction films of the era that are often comically bad due to the cheesy low-rent special effects, costumes and props. These films frequently failed because they attempted to make big-budget productions with a fraction of the budget as if nobody would notice the considerable lack of production values.

Jumping ahead into the 1970s, when low-budget grindhouse films found a loyal audience at drive-ins, the relatively low-budget Halloween (1978) spawned hundreds and hundreds of low-budget knockoffs and sequels. Of course, the 1970s also saw John Sayles (who cut his teeth by writing low-budget screenplays for Roger Corman) release his first film, The Return of the Secaucus Seven (1979), which kind of set the stage for the independent film boom in the 1980s, where we were introduced to The Coen Bros., Jim Jarmusch,

Spike Lee and Steven Soderbergh, all working within the parameters of low budgets.

Of course, while maybe not considered by many to be an independent film in the conventional sense, the 1970s also gave us Rocky (1976). When, then D-list actor Sylvester Stallone, unhappy with the roles he was being offered, decided to write a vehicle for himself and then almost single-handedly willed it into production, he basically cast the mold for countless independent films that came in the generations that followed with some variation on the mantra "Make Your Own Damn Movie." Now, Rocky means a lot of different things to a lot of people around the world. For a film geek growing up in Philly, the thought that this virtual nobody could write a screenplay set in Philadelphia, shoot it in Philadelphia ("huh, you mean that not all movies are produced in L.A.?"), see it become a big hit and win the Oscar for Best Picture was mind-blowing, exhilarating and inspiring.

So, low-budget independent filmmaking is nothing new, but, in the past 40 years or so, it has become more visible, less conventionally fringe and even has a dedicated audience of people who proclaim themselves "indie film fans." For me personally, much in the way fans of indie, underground music are always on the lookout for the next great artist nobody has ever heard of, I am always looking for low-budget, low-profile, often lo-fi independent films that tend to fly way below the radar—and there are many of them out there. Indeed, it seems like everyone's grandmothers and neighbors are making films.

Filmmaking has become democratized. Basically, anyone can do it and many of them are. While, yes, this democratization has opened doors for fresh, original voices to make films and share their ideas in ways that would not have been imaginable 40 years ago, it also means that there are not only a whole lot of really bad movies being produced and distributed, there are even more really bad but possibly really good movies that have not been finished because the filmmakers ran out of resources. Too many filmmakers rush into production without fully thinking things through. They aim for ambitious projects that ultimately fall out of their reach. The trick, and the point of this book, is for filmmakers to have a firm grasp on just how far their reach goes and to then reverse engineer their projects accordingly.

Low-budget filmmaking is not rocket science. There are really only a handful of concepts that you need to grasp. That said, losing weight, on a fundamental level, generally comes down to burning more calories than you consume, but it is often a little more complicated. So, similarly, when it comes to making low-budget films, it is a little more complicated than not spending as much money.

Then what can you afford? Yes, lots of people like to see stunts, amazing sets, locations and special effects, but a producer can spend millions of dollars on those things and still have a film that falls flat if it is missing the heart and soul of a film: sympathetic or, at least, compelling characters who do interesting things. Good stories come from good characters.

Conveniently, human beings come with an imagination built-in; it is not an added feature like a moonroof. If, for whatever reasons, you cannot come up with a good, fully formed idea for a movie on your own, you should find—and hopefully pay/defer pay or barter with—someone who can: a talented, if not incredibly experienced, screenwriter to write a screenplay. You can then afford to pay, defer pay or barter with a crew to shoot this film and actors to play these characters. If you do the things that this book discusses, you will be able to find affordable places for these actors to perform the scenes in the screenplay.

People make low-budget films for all kinds of reasons: some cannot raise large amounts of money and some like a lo-fi/skin of the teeth kind of mentality in production. What we are seeing more and more of is filmmakers who score with a modestly produced low-budget indie hit are being tapped to write and/or direct major, big-budget releases. From Safety Not Guaranteed (2012) director Colin Trevorrow and screenwriter Derek Connolly going from that film to Jurassic World (2015) and steadfastly indie-minded writer-director Alex Ross Perry getting hired to write 2018's Christopher Robin to Ryan Fleck and Anna Bolden moving from intimate small films like Half Nelson (2006) and Sugar (2008) to Captain Marvel (2019), more and more, filmmakers with humble roots are jumping to the head of the class and getting big-budget gigs based on the strength of their early, low-budget work. Can you believe that Chloe Zhao has gone from Songs My Brothers Taught Me (2015), The Rider (2017) and Nomadland (2020) to Marvel's The Eternals (2021)? I can.

Similarly, in the new era of "prestige television," there have been a number of shows coming directly from one-time indie feature filmmakers. The trend might have started with Lena Dunham, who had made some shorts, her medium-length film Creative Nonfiction (2009), and her feature Tiny Furniture (2010) before creating Girls (2012–2017). Now, we have shows like Search Party (2016–present) which was created by Sarah-Violet Bliss (who had co-directed one feature) and Charles Rogers following the success of their film Fort Tilden (2014) and Love Life (2020) by Sam Boyd, who had written and directed one feature In A Relationship (2018) before creating the show.

Let's discuss what this book is not. Importantly, this book is not an Introduction to Screenwriting book, it assumes some degree of experience with the form. Though, by nature, I have to touch on it, this book is not about structure, character development, dialogue and formatting. There are ample places to learn about those elements of the craft. This book is really about hacks and strategies for writing screenplays for micro-budget films that use limited resources to their advantage as well as how to avoid some of the pitfalls that micro-budget filmmakers often encounter (and too often ignore) at the screenplay/concept stage. This book assumes that, on some level, you know how to write a story for the screen but that you might need to learn how to specifically design a story that can be produced on a low budget.

This book explores the techniques and special considerations that go into writing for low budgets. By presenting case studies of successful low-budget films, writers, directors and producers will have a solid foothold to stand on when starting out on a new project.

By laying out the concepts central to conceiving and writing a story suitable for production on a low budget that I have learned in over 30 years of study as well as in the production of my own low-budget feature and including interviews from some of the most acclaimed independent writer–directors working today as well as newer talent brewing just below the surface, I hope to enlighten, educate and inspire others who dream of making films.

I think I always thought I would grow up and out of this silly dream of making films for a living, but, despite ample inspiration, it still has not happened.

# 1

# KNOW YOUR LIMITATIONS

Orson Welles once said, "The enemy of art is the absence of limitations."

Not long ago, someone asked me "What do you call a person who makes a film all by himself?"

My answer: "Resourceful."

When my daughters were younger, they were really into doing original plays for the family. These productions usually consisted of them playing the major roles and their dolls taking on all of the supporting parts on makeshift sets that were meant to represent elaborate luxurious or fantastical worlds. After one of their shows, in a case of what might be considered questionable parenting, I congratulated them but suggested that they try to come up with a show that did not require casting inanimate objects or using unrealistic sets. What they came up with kind of blew me away. For their next show, they had a total of four characters and the story was set in the contemporary, everyday world. In the first act, the two of them played two characters and, in the next act, they played two different characters, but all of them drove the narrative and related to each other in a coherent way. They really pulled it off; it was inventive, ambitious, successful and, most importantly, resourceful. They took stock of their assets and crafted a play that was brilliantly designed to work with what was available to them, within their constraints,

DOI: 10.4324/9781003138969-2

not against them. They even composed and performed the music. Over 15 years later, the memory of that experience has never faded and, in fact, moved to the forefront of my mind as I wrote this book.

When I spoke with director, writer, producer and actress Meosha Bean, she had just been asked to make a $100,000 film for a distributor who already had a screenplay. I asked about what she looks for in a screenplay for a film that will be produced on such a small budget.

Meosha Bean:

> I look for a lot of things. One, if I liked the script and it spoke to me, was it something that I really wanted to do. Number two, what is it, what are we trying to say, what are we talking about, what message are we trying to put across for the audience? Sure, of course, I'm trying to do the whole Jordan Peele thing, where it is like, you watch a horror movie, but you're like, "Oh, wow, that was creepy. But also, it made me think." I got a script recently and it takes place in this house and I like the challenges of having three people in one location. It's not "use the space I need", it is "Let's use the whole house, let's use everything, the backyard, the front yard, the driveway."
>
> This distributor reached out to a filmmaker friend of mine and they basically gave him $100,000 to make this feature. And so, he calls me because I've done so many independent films. It is fun location scouting and looking for places where we want to make this happen. And of course, Los Angeles is very expensive. So it goes back to asking for favors, friends that say "Hey, I have a friend that has a really nice house, and I'm like, 'this could be this is doable." He's like, "Use my place."

Lawrence Michael Levine is a screenwriter, a director, a producer and an actor who frequently collaborates with his wife, screenwriter, director, producer, actress and editor Sophia Takal. We spoke just before the release of his film Black Bear (2020), which at times, feels like a fictional account of the production of Takal's micro-budget delight Always Shine (2016).

When I was in college, I watched Cassavetes, I watched all of it. But I think Faces (1968) was the first one I watched. And I was like, "Oh wait, you can make movies about real life that feel really real and depict people as they actually behave and act and comment on that?" And I thought, "Okay, well I can't do this." Like bullshit movies that seem too big. Like I can't make, I don't know, whatever was popular at the time, like The Matrix (1999). I don't see myself making that kind of movie. It's just kind of knowing your limits. But in my case, there was like, actually no desire to do anything bigger. Look, this movie is holding my interest. And it's just people in very everyday situations and places and outfits. And I could maybe do something like this. And then I was desperate to learn how to do it because I didn't know how to. I knew there was some kind of approach. I knew this stuff was really interesting that was going on in Faces but I didn't really know how to accomplish effects like that.

So I was desperate to learn how to learn everything that Cassavetes seemed to know. So he was an actor. He started out as an actor. I read everything I could get my hands on, Ray Carney's books, for example. And whatever was available at the time about him. And, and that turned me on to other people like Mike Leigh. So, I got really into Mike Leigh, who similarly makes all that stuff that is pretty simple in terms of setting and, and there's nothing fancy there.

You know, these were people who were making films that were drawing energy from different sources than your typical Hollywood action film. You know, it was very obvious to me that something rich was happening going on here. I just didn't understand how to do it, but I felt like I could get there. So, I got into Mike Leigh, and then another guy that Ray Carney was writing about, Tom Noonan. So, I watched Tom Noonan films, and I really liked them. And I was just really looking for guidance, and I was looking for a mentor and I had no idea that Tom

Noonan, at that time, was this remote figure as Mike Leigh is to me now. I had no idea that Tom Noonan would ever be somebody that I would meet or anything but one day, I was walking around the village, and I came across a sign in front of a building that said, Tom Noonan actually teaches acting, writing, directing, I don't know exactly the time said, and I was like, "Holy shit, this is crazy. Tom Noonan teaches classes, and I could take them." And, you know, Tom Noonan made these two movies where it's just people sitting around, you know, talking and I think they work brilliantly. So, I got into his class. And it really set me on the path that I'm still on today, because I learned the specific kind of techniques and approaches to writing, writing drama, really.

Back to my earlier point, do it for fun. I would never tell you to not write out your ideas. I feel that anytime we sit down to write, we have the potential to become better writers by practicing our craft. Also, it is just so much fun to create these worlds and think about them. To me, there are few better feelings than that of looking forward to writing, the feeling you get when you're so in love with an idea that you think about even when you're not writing.

Now, if you have written a really great screenplay that's been calibrated to be produced with a modest budget, you might have a better chance. I had a very low-budget screenplay optioned by a production company that was looking to make a feature after years in the business of producing commercials, reality TV, music videos and so on.

Step 1, painful as it might be, is to be conscious of the kinds of films that are problematic to produce on a low budget. Shifting to the right mindset is the most important part of the job. Start small. Do your research.

Noam Kroll is a filmmaker whose 2020 film Psychosynthesis was made on a modest budget. On his podcast Show, Don't Tell, he regularly offers filmmaking advice based on his own experiences. He takes a philosophical approach to having limitations.

When it comes to writing, everyone sort of says minimal locations, minimal cast, there's all these rules. And, and there's obviously a reason that people say that and, and all those parameters can certainly help you on your way to making your film more feasible. However, the way that I like to approach it is I like to think about what's something that you can do on a smaller budget that you wouldn't be able to do on a bigger budget. So sort of looking at ways to embrace the limitations. So for example, a certain subject matters, certain points of view, certain characters that you want to explore might not really be feasible on a larger canvas, because if you have a bunch of investors putting $8 million into your indie movie, they're going to obviously want to have a say, they're going to want to make sure that it's as marketable as possible and rightfully so when you're dealing with $20,000 or $50,000, that you sort of cobbled together to make your movie that opens up the door for a lot of the creative exploration that you literally wouldn't be able to do, if you had more money, unless you were just independently wealthy. So I think that's sort of always my biggest point that I try to get across to filmmakers is, look for the thing. What's the unique advantage that you actually have by not having money? What's the story that you could tell on a smaller budget that you wouldn't be able to, if you had more money. You could take more risks.

Here is the thing, screenwriting is not rocket science. Anyone can learn the basics of structure and formatting. That does not necessarily mean that their screenplays will be good. What is more important is that screenplays are not just good (well, okay, better than good), but they are producible and, in a relatively perfect world, if produced, stand a chance of breaking even financially if not providing a return on investment.

In the early 1990s, I was a few years out of film school, reading everything I could get my hands on about making low-budget independent films. I kept seeing film magazine ads for Dov S-S Simens' 2-Film School, a weekend seminar that promised to unlock the mysteries of how to make a feature for next to nothing. Simens worked for Roger Corman, one of the undisputed titans of low-budget, independent films that countless filmmakers cite as an inspiration. So, I took the workshop in early 1992 and hung on every word. I still remember that one of Simens' parting lines was "Rent a house in the woods, hire a bunch of kids, chop 'em up and you've got a movie." It is a model that has endured for generations and even spawned some good movies.

At this point, the model for micro-budget filmmaking is nothing new and fairly well-known: few locations and few characters, no exterior shots at night if possible, minimal special effects or stunts. Frequently, this approach leaves us with films about people talking to each other. There are few cheaper ways to make a film than just shooting people talking to each other. The problem that many film-makers attempting this kind of shoot is that scenes are often longer and "talkier" than average and, unfortunately, more static and stagy. No matter how ingenious the plot is and how sparkling the dialogue might be, there is great danger of the film becoming visually dull. So, one of the primary goals of this book is to look for ways to keep micro-budget films genuinely cinematic (which comes from the root kinetic, meaning motion), visually active by building activity into the project at the screenplay level.

Sure, you say, what about My Dinner With Andre (1981), that was just two guys talking? If you can write something on the level of My Dinner With Andre, please do, I would love to see it. Sure, you say, we can just do an Aaron Sorkin walk-and-talk to keep things active visually. Well, can you? Do you, as a writer, know what goes into producing a walk-and-talk, how much time, effort and expense of your resources will be required? If you do and you think it is the right way to go, then go for it. Filmmaking is 90% problem-solving, figuring out how to tell a good story with a camera.

Remember, when we talk about cinema, movies, we are talking about motion pictures. Cameras can both capture motion and move themselves, so it is critically important to keep these elements of cin-ema in mind. Orson Welles really understood the power of the cam-era and his films are filled with stunning compositions of characters in motion as well as camera movement back and forth, up and down the frame and, of course, as famously seen in the opening sequence to Touch Of Evil (1958), a frame that can move with action. No, on a micro-budget film, you might not be able to afford dollies and cranes, but there are many ways to move a camera and, when appropriate for the film, a production should remember to utilize them.

When I spoke with writer-director Alex Ross Perry, the topic of writing for your limitations came up,

> When you're writing the script, how much do you already know? I'm not going to write a location that can take me all this time and money to find. I wrote a movie for this location. I don't need to go find it. And I wrote a scene right for this aesthetic decision. I'm not going to have to think of that later. And a lot of the work as a writer is just solving every production problem and every question while you are writing.

DG:  But on this level, you have to reverse engineer and say "What do I have access to? You know, my parents own a laundromat," and you set a movie in a laundromat instead of the other way around where you think of locations while you're writing.

ARP:  "That's always been my method, at least on those earlier films. And still, no matter what I'm aiming for, on whatever script or project I'm currently attempting to unlock. That's my background, that's my education that I gave myself, I cannot detach myself from that, because every attempt I've ever made, to just shoot for the moon in terms of locations or resources, those end up being the scripts that do not get made or get changed the most, to the point that it's not the thing anymore. And those are hard-earned lessons, but they just came about by making two movies, both for under $25,000. And this still again, from those two movies. I remember I was outlining Her Smell (2018). And I called both the wardrobe designer and the makeup designer that I'd worked with on my three previous films, and said, 'If I'm writing scenes that have seven women completely styled from head to toe, how bad is that logjam going to be at the start of the day?' What they both said was, 'Here's the budget we're going to need to be able to get that size of a cast looking the way you want this movie to look out of wardrobe, hair and makeup in about 90 minutes every day, so that you have a full day to shoot. If you can provide us with this budget, and this many hands in our department, then there's nothing to worry about.' So I then had the freedom to continue writing as I wanted, and then telling everybody I already checked with these department heads, they asked for a department of seven instead of department of three, and we need to give it to them or else we're never going to make our days. And everybody was very amazed that that problem had been solved before it ever became a problem. And that is a lesson you only get if you're writing a movie you're going to make for $20,000 and calling people while writing it and saying, will you be in a movie? If I write a character right now? I want to do a scene with this car, you have that car? Can we borrow it? And then you just solve this stuff while you're sitting by yourself."

If I would also make a movie the size of Queen of Earth (2015). If we were saying, post pandemic, our only option to make a movie is going to be making something in one location where the actors wear their own clothes. I would be writing that movie, but I did not, Her Smell was not that story. So therefore, everything had to be thought of while writing. And again, that's a movie that far outpaces the parameters of what you're discussing, the blessing is it was only possible because of how I made my earlier movies.

So, it is critical to be aware of your limitations and your resources. I spoke with writer-producer-director, fellow screenwriting professor and host of the Scriptcake podcast Lovinder Gill on the topic and he said,

So whenever you're shooting a movie, you're gonna have some limitations. Whenever you're writing a movie, even if you want to write something in a particular genre, that genre comes with limitations. But a low budget does not mean you cannot be creative. In fact, it means you have to be creative. "I don't have a lot of money?" That's fine. That doesn't mean you can't be creative. If you look at a simple sequence, where two people are discussing something, (some) writers will put that in a restaurant. Why? Because that's where people talk. Right? Okay. But that doesn't mean or say anything about the characters. You know, in fact, you're gonna have to pay for a restaurant and pay for all the people in the background and pay for a whole bunch of other stuff. People are thinking about the parameters of a story that they want to write and they will limit themselves beyond their actual limitations.

As an example of effectively utilizing available resources, take a look at the Bad Ben (2016–present) franchise. Never heard of it? You are not alone, but you might be shocked to find out what a rabid fan base it has. It is one thing to make a micro-budget film in your own house with available resources, but to make nine films like this—in the same location—for a grand total of around $20,000 is a whole other story.

Written, produced, shot and edited by my friend Nigel Bach, Bad Ben cost $300 to make and then another $1300 went into marketing. Bach willed the film into existence when his original plans went awry after his cast dropped out right before shooting. He improvised a monologue, cast himself and designed the entire film to be shot on home security cameras and cell phones. Bach is the only actor in the film and made up 99.9% of the crew. Eight Bad Ben films later—and #9 just wrapped—the series has made back its budget many times over. No, it's not as well-known as The Blair Witch Project (1999) or the Paranormal Activity (2007–2015) series, but proportionately, it has to be considered a success especially because it never had a theatrical run with a big advertising campaign or press and, bottom-line, the director makes a living on these films.

Nigel Bach: I'd been writing screenplays and trying to pitch them. And people would say to me, "Why don't you make your own movies?" And the thing they didn't realize, because you own a camera, does it mean you can make Avatar? You know, you have limitations? I reverse engineered my movie. I've heard this saying "when the only tool you have is a hammer, you tend to treat everything like a nail." So I knew that I had a camera, but it still was prosumer at best. I had to think "what could I make with what I had?" I had a hammer, what could be my nail and I knew that a found footage type film that's supposed to look like something that was shot on a regular camera or even security cameras? That was something that was my nail, and I had the hammer to do that.

Someone once asked me if it is possible to make a feature for $100. As much as I would try to dissuade anyone from making a film on that budget, I cannot say that it is impossible. If you reverse engineer your production, you can, conceivably, make a movie for $100. Is it going to be a movie with state-of-the-art cinematography, effects, acting, sets and costumes? Probably not. But, honestly, if you really think everything through and become incredibly resourceful and, if you write a great screenplay for it, one that embraces the limitations of your budget, it is possible to produce a $100.00 feature film.

So, what do I mean by "reverse engineer" and "embrace the limitations"? Indie film 101 is founded on this principle: two to four characters, two to four locations. First, unlike most movies with decent budgets, for a micro-budget film, you should take stock of your available resources. Do your parents own a deli? If so, you write a screenplay where 90% of the story takes place in a deli. If you know anyone who owns a spaceship, then you can make a science fiction film. Next, cast the best, most reliable actors willing to work for little-to-no money.

When I say "embrace the limitations," I mean "don't agonize over production values." Yes, make the film look as good as you can but you are unlikely to be able to afford especially nice art direction, costume design, stunts and sets, so write a screenplay that does not require them. There are few things worse than a movie that looks low rent because the filmmakers tried to shoot for high-end settings, locations and props but used cheesy substitutes. Make a movie about "regular" people who don't have fancy cars or lavish homes—unless you have unlimited access to those things.

Noam Kroll told me:

> My biggest point that I try to get across to filmmakers is to look for the thing. What's the unique advantage that you actually have by not having money? What's the story that you could tell on a smaller budget that you wouldn't be able to, if you had more money, you could take more risks. You could be more experimental with blending genres, if you're making a commentary on something, that there's an angle to it. I think about exploring that because the number one thing that ultimately will help your micro budget film is the concept and is differentiating what you're doing from the $10 million movie to $50 million movie. But I do think that you're better off when you embrace the limitations, as opposed to try to, uh, pretend that they're not there and try to make your production or your, even the writing of your film resemble a much larger budget feature, because then you're not really taking advantage of the smaller canvas that you're working on.
>
> The last, possibly most important point to me is, above anything else: write a great screenplay with well developed characters.

Robert Greene works primarily in documentaries, but he has also edited films by Alex Ross Perry and Bob Byington, among others. As a director, he first entered my radar with the astonishing narrative-documentary hybrid Kate Plays Christine (2016). He reaffirms the philosophy that

> with micro budget films, you really do have to factor in the production technique. I mean, you have to know what your parameters are and how you're going to execute when you have no money. I think any time you're writing screenplays, especially with budget limitations, with time limitations, and those go hand in hand, I think it's really a matter of just setting up so the vision of the overall film needs to match and lean into the strengths, not the weaknesses. You need to write with a mind of

where you're going to shoot, you need to write a mind of who you're going to have in it, you need to write with a mind of like, what are your days going to look like filming it, and those need to be integrated and, and they need to relate to each other strongly.

Jim Byrkit co-wrote Rango (2011) and has had a solid career doing things like concept art on some of the Pirates of the Caribbean films, but it was his 2013 feature writing-directing debut Coherence, a mind-bending lo-fi sci-fi psychological thriller made for $50,000 and shot in five days that got my attention. Byrkit told me that

> When you don't have resources, it forces you to be creative and look around. And what do you have and I had a living room, and I had some friends that could act and I had a camera. It's surprising what you will come up with when you're forced to deal with the resources at hand. You come up against the limits of your imagination.

When you read movie reviews, what is being criticized? Usually, a movie review says who made the film, who's in it and if the story is any good. Rarely, do you see a review that criticizes the sound effects editing or the best boy. People want to see a good story and, at this level of filmmaking, the screenplay is the least expensive element of the production. It costs next to nothing—sometimes even less—to write a good screenplay, so take your time, be smart about it and never forget that you are making a $100–$100,000 film but bend over backward to make sure that your screenplay is not as good as it can be, it is ten times better than it should be.

Audiences will forgive low-production values if they are wrapped up in a good story. Nobody will forgive a bad story no matter how much the film cost to make.

# 2

# GETTING REAL

Plain and simple, you can have a $200,000,000 budget, a top-notch crew, a cast full of A-listers and the best special effects in the business but, the vast bulk of the time, if you do not have a really good screenplay, the chances of making a really good film are usually pretty small. On the flip side, a micro-budget film with technical limitations but a strong enough screenplay and great cast stands a pretty strong chance of becoming a decent film.

Someone started telling me about the series of screenplays he had written and the cinematic universe he had created. He asked me "How do you pitch it to Hollywood?"

As gently and diplomatically as possible, I said something to the effect of "You don't." I tempered that statement with "Do it for fun."

I get it; everyone likes movies and quite a few people dream of having a career in film as a director, a cinematographer, an actor or a writer. Films are the art form closest to dreams; we have little movies that play in our heads every night. When I wrote my first screenplay at 13 years old, I could see it so vividly in my mind, it was wonderful to sit down and write (longhand) and imagine the world of my film. So, I get it, world building, dreaming up elaborate scenarios, dynamic characters and imagining who would play them is fun. It is when you start to take it too seriously and think about trying to get

DOI: 10.4324/9781003138969-3

the film produced that the fun can disappear faster than you can say "smash cut."

If you are talking about a big-budget, FX-heavy series of films like Avatar (2009), Star Wars (1977) or The Avengers (2012), look into the history of those projects. Cameron was a massively successful filmmaker before he introduced the Avatar universe. Lucas was a moderately successful filmmaker when he started Star Wars. The MCU is a pre-sold commodity because the films are based on characters who have been popular for decades. Getting them produced was considerably easier for them because they were established entities.

If you are not an industry insider with a track record of success, you might find a lot of closed doors if you have written a location/ large cast/stunts and special effects intensive screenplay, unless you have secured financing. If you have the money to make that kind of film, you will easily find a production company to make it for/with you. The days where a "regular" person could send out a screenplay to a production company and have even a slim chance of getting it made are largely gone.

Let's get real about selling screenplays and creating cinematic universes. Something like 94% of all screenwriting jobs are assignments for-hire: the producers generate a project they can afford and hire a writer. It's usually not the other way around where a writer generates a project and then goes looking for people to finance it—especially if it is a big-budget, effects-heavy production featuring unfamiliar characters and worlds.

Unless you are working in the business now, doing well and have a good reputation, you are probably talking about submitting a spec screenplay. Hollywood receives about 100,000 spec screenplays every year and usually less than 100 are sold. The odds are so high. What spec or under-the-radar scripts have done well recently? BlaKK-Klansman (2018) and A Quiet Place (2018) were both reportedly discovered on The Black List. Whether or not they were truly specs, I'm not sure. I can't think of a "universe" or series of films that began as a spec. Okay, Cameron was not a big director when he made The Terminator (1984). Technically, maybe the Rocky franchise sort of counts but, again, the first film was essentially a grungy, low-budget indie.

No matter what you think of him as a person, Woody Allen has been nominated for 16 Best Original Screenplay Oscars and won three times. In Eric Lax's Conversations with Woody Allen, the film-maker says,

> If you have a good script and you shoot it in a stupid way, badly lit and badly shot, you can still have a successful movie . . . Whereas, if you have bad material, if the writing is not good, you can shoot the eyes out of it every way and, most of the time, no matter what style you bring to the film, it doesn't work.

I believe that very few filmmakers gather financing, resources, equipment, crew, cast, then just turn on the camera and wait to see what happens. The same approach should apply to films made on any budget. I seriously doubt that any films went into production without something resembling a screenplay, but I have heard of plenty of films that started shooting with a screenplay that needed more work; was clearly not camera-ready and resulted in a less than satisfying film. Do you remember Sydney Pollack's 2005 film The Interpreter? You are forgiven if it does not ring a bell, it was not well received. Reportedly, star Sean Penn convinced Nicole Kidman to take a role in it even though the problematic screenplay was still undergoing major rewrites, assuring her that everything would work out in the end. Sure, it actually made decent money worldwide, but, on Rotten Tomatoes, the film has a 57% critical score and 54% audience score with the consensus summed up by "A polished and intelligent thriller, though marred by plot implausibilities." Okay, "polished and intelligent" sound like compliments to the production and screenplay (which was, in part, written by superstar screenwriters Steve Zaillian and Scott Frank), but, to me, if you are part of a studio machine that is spending $80,000,000 on a film, it should not be "marred by plot implausibilities." Yes, maybe the plot logic was sound in the screenplay and lost in the editing room but, what should come first here, a sensible plot or the running time? Why would you sign on to a film without first making sure that the screenplay was, at least, mostly airtight?

To me, on a major film, where costs can be more than $1,000,000 a day, the idea of going into production without an airtight screenplay seems irresponsible, irrational and like a recipe for disaster or, at least, mediocrity, but it happens all the time. It was reported rather publicly that the screenplay for Joker (2019) was being rewritten every day. I saw Stephen King working on revisions to the Pet Sematary screenplay on set. Steven Spielberg once said "You can't start a movie by having the attitude that the script is finished, because if you think the script is finished, your movie is finished before the first day of shooting" because things usually change in production and post-production, but going into production without a relatively coherent sense of what happens in the story is asking for trouble. I'm not saying that filmmakers should not be open to sudden fits of inspiration during the shoot, things change and people come up with new ideas all of the time.

Between writing the first draft and the second draft of this book, I went off to produce Seclusion. Now, I have had screenplays radically altered in production and it took me a while to adjust to the reality that my words were not written in stone. In a theater, the words of the playwright are usually treated like a holy text; they are not altered without the input of the writer. Not so in film. While the WGA sets a limit on the number of screenwriters who can be credited on a film, there are often as many as dozens of writers who contribute to the final screenplay. In the case of Seclusion, we had seven or eight drafts from the original writer and we tinkered with it but, once on set, things shifted. Toward the end of the shoot, scenes were getting cut, lines were being added and, most importantly, because the chemistry between our leads was so strong, we began to emphasize a romance element of the story that was not in the screenplay. Now it was my turn to be one of the guys altering someone else's screenplay in production rather than the other way around. Because the story can be in flux and evolve during production, it has been said that there is the screenplay you write, the screenplay you shoot and the screenplay you edit. The lesson is that you have to be flexible, ready to solve problems on set and be open to inspiration. We were happy with the Seclusion screenplay when we went into production, but inspiration struck and we were ready to adjust as needed.

So, I hate to sound cranky, but I have seen a lot of low-budget indie films made by people who know how to shoot well, light well, edit well, do special effects well but cannot tell an interesting, compelling story and that should not be the case. It is really not that hard to come up with a story for a film. Yes, it is hard to come up with an original, intelligent story for a film, but so many of you are just aiming to make basic, ordinary films anyway and there is nothing wrong with that if the story is strong, the structure is sound and the characters are compelling.

If you are reading this book, there is a good chance that you have an interest in writing and maybe producing a film on an extremely low budget. The average major studio release costs around $80,000,000 to produce. In Hollywood, anything under $50,000,000 is considered low budget. Even some small-scale producers will not consider any project with a budget less than $10,000,000. The reality is that most of us are going to have a hard time raising even $1,000,000 to make a film. It's been said that filmmaking is 90% fundraising (I know that I just said "filmmaking is 90% problem solving" in the last chapter so, for the sake of argument, let's call lack of funds a problem that needs to be solved) and there is something to that way of thinking.

My feeling has always been "Why write a symphony if you do not have an orchestra to play it? Why not write for a string quartet instead?" Writing a micro-budget film is writing for a string quartet.

I read screenplays all the time. I grade them for students and I read them for filmmaker friends who come to me for advice. From time to time, someone I do not know reaches out to me and asks me to read a screenplay for them or to ask for suggestions on how to get into film production.

Recently, a stranger asked me to read a screenplay for a film that they want to make. The guy can write and the film would be really cool if he could make it. The project involves many locations (from city to beach, east coast to west coast), lots of characters, stunts and special effects. So, like many of the screenplays I read, the "if he could make it" factor is where a lot of beginning filmmakers struggle and I offered him the following advice:

> The bottom-line with this screenplay is the bottom-line. As-is, I think it would be expensive and complicated to produce. Now someone else might read it and jump at the chance to take on this challenge. My orientation has been towards really simple, Micro Budget films because, of course, they don't cost that much to make and they don't cost so much to make because they usually involve small casts and few locations.
>
> Unless you have very deep pockets, have connections to investors or are really good at fundraising, the big trick to filmmaking from my perspective is coming up with a screenplay that you can actually make, that is not going to require a lot of set-ups in different places, complicated effects or stunts and a cast and crew of thousands, hundreds or even dozens.

I came to screenwriting after film school and working on the crews of movies, music videos, infomercials, etc. so, for better or worse, I write with production in mind. I want people to pick up my screenplays and say "I want to make this film and I think I can make this film.

So my advice would be to do what you are doing, get out into your local film community if you have one, meet people, offer to work on their films, make connections, get hands-on experience and build up a network of people who can help you with your stuff."

It doesn't cost much to write a screenplay, but a screenplay on its own is nothing—remember it's like writing a symphony but not having an orchestra to perform it. With today's technology, anyone can make a film and plenty of people are trying to make films. I have seen plenty of people start films and not be able to finish them. I have seen some great films made with simple, inexpensive equipment, and I have seen a lot of really bad films. The point here is to know what you're doing as well as you can before you actually go out and try to do it.

Filmmaker and novelist Polly Schattel has made three features and had a number of screenplays optioned. We spoke about the way to approach the writing of a film on this level.

> The films are so writing intensive, because you don't have to rely on special effects and great cinematography. You just have to have good words. You start looking for these scenarios, and start thinking, "What can I dig out of this scenario?" For instance, on my second film, Alison (2009), I had just bought a new house. So I knew I had the run of the place. So you look for these little complications that you can flesh out. But necessarily, of course, these are indie films, rather than a super-hero blockbuster, these are smaller, more character based dramas. You can't afford to do flying and shooting and blowing up. You sort of work backwards from what you actually have. You know, for instance, on my third film, Quiet River (2015), I had a really talented actor who lived in the weirdest little tiny cabin ever. And she basically gave me the run of it, she said we can shoot in here alone. So we literally fashioned that story backwards out of what we had available to us and we created this thing and she helped me to create this narrative of a Ted Kaczynski-like troubled senior who was living in this small cabin. So you work backwards from what you have available to you. And that's really where you start.

In 1999, I was teaching film classes at my old high school. The students and I were trying to come up with an idea for a film that we could shoot start-to-finish during a class period. Quickly we determined that we should set it in real time, have one primary location and have new characters come to it rather than moving characters to another location. We never wound up making that film, but the idea and the approach to production stayed with me and ultimately turned into the feature I shot in 2013, Stomping Ground (2016).

Around the same time, I was reviewing films for Home Media Entertainment Magazine and became one of the primary reviewers for IndieTalk.com. In that capacity, I saw a lot of movies and, in the case of reviewing for IndieTalk, I saw a lot of films that had not (and would not) get distribution, some of them really good and some of them truly terrible. The bottom-line for me was that the "digital revolution" had arrived and that everyone was making micro-budget films. I figured, "I should try to make a micro-budget film like everyone else, spend a modest amount of money and, if the film never gets distributed and I lose some money, I can live with it."

In one of my IndieTalk reviews, I bashed the filmmakers for having a terrible screenplay, but I wrote that I didn't mean to single them out, that bad screenplays are a real issue in many of the films that I reviewed for that site.

I know that the technology at our hands is amazing, cool, etc., that the possibilities are virtually endless these days. There are so many great cameras out there now—I have seen most of the hottest cameras and accessories out there up close and they really are all that they are cracked up to be. There are also plenty of really decent, moderately priced cameras out there that do perfectly acceptable work. High-quality post-production seems to be at everyone's fingertips.

So, what is the problem? Too many of "us" in the indie world (well, the mainstream film world, too) seem to be too focused on the technology, so much so that the foundation of a film is being ignored. I implore you to put your camera down, step away from your software and invest in what I consider essential filmmaking equipment: a good book on screenwriting. But, that's just me. Some filmmakers interviewed for this book might disagree.

For $25.00 or less, you can buy a book that will open your eyes to the magic of plotting out a story. I know that a lot of technical, creative people are intimidated by screenwriting that they find it mysterious and daunting to have to learn "the formula" and the formatting, but it really helps.

Even if you just learn the basics, it can make your films and your approach to filmmaking so much better. Learn the basic concepts of structure, conflicts, what makes a strong main character, etc., and it might be revolutionary to you.

So, by all means, while you are waiting for your Blackmagic URSA Mini Pro to arrive, pick up a good book on screenwriting, learn the basics and apply them to your next film, please.

I get it, why read a book when you could be making a movie? I have had to work to fight against my resistance to conventions. When I read Syd Field's classic Screenplay as an idealistic but cynical and opinionated young 20-something back in the 1980s I couldn't get through it, I was so disgusted by the idea that the art of cinema could be boiled down to a simple formula, X, Y and Z by page 10, An Act Break on or around page 30, Act 2A, mid-point, Act 2B, another Act Break on page 60 or 90 depending on how long the film is, etc. I reread the book in my slightly more serene late 30s after having had a couple of professional screenwriting gigs and came to embrace it warmly.

Okay, still not convinced that the screenplay is not the most important part of a film, don't want to read a book on screenwriting and learn some of the basics? Fine, just do me a favor, find someone who has read a book on screenwriting and ask them to write a movie for you.

Indiewire.com recently published its list of the Best Undistributed Films in their year-end critics poll. More than 160 critics voted. Altogether, around 275 films made the list. Granted, some of these films have gotten distribution deals that have not yet been announced, but, according to the site, the top five films, those that were mentioned the most, do not, at this time, have deals for theatrical distribution.

Everywhere I turn, I hear about an actress or actor friend shooting this film or that film and everyone seems to be a director or a producer promoting their new film as they are shooting it—sometimes even long before they start shooting. I understand that marketing buzz, building brand awareness and consumer interest is the name of the game but it sometimes seems like that is the only thing happening. I hear about all these films in the pre-production, then production stage and then what, they're gone?

So many of these films just seem to disappear without getting much, if any kind of "proper" release—much less a theatrical run.

Maybe I am old school in thinking that having a movie shown in a movie theater is the ultimate goal. However, film is a public art, it succeeds when people see it and I am not just talking about having a screening at a bar for friends and family.

Still, for me, a theatrical screening—even if it is just at a film festival or two—is the gold standard. Maybe I am small minded in thinking like this, but, if I bust my butt and break the bank to make a film, it means more to me to have people make an effort to go see it in a theater than it does to know that they are clicking a button on their computer and watching it while they are checking their email.

For some people, having a screening of their film—maybe renting out a screen at the local art-house theater—for friends and family is as good as it will ever get. For some people, the gold standard is breaking even, maybe even having something to hand over to their investors.

If you really want to know my feelings on the matter, I want to make a film that does "well enough" critically and/or commercially to inspire someone to back me on another film and the film after that one and the film after that one and so on.

I have been watching the business of indie films and how they get to their audience almost as long as I have been watching indie films. In the "anyone can make a film" era, saying that you are making a film does not carry much weight with me. Telling me that your film screened at a reputable festival, got picked up by a distributor with muscle or even, yes, that it's been downloaded/whatevered 500 times is going to impress me.

So, whether or not my thinking is stuck in the past is less of an issue for me.

The Hollywood Economist Blogspot estimates that, worldwide, there are 4000–5000 independent features made each year and, of that number, only 2% will be purchased for distribution. Making a film is half of the battle, maybe not even half. Getting people to see your film is the real trick.

Today, anyone can make a movie and, from my perspective, far too many people are making mediocre movies and, not that I am a math whiz by any stretch or into odds and probabilities, it just seems that the more movies that are out there, the more chances for more of these movies to be bad increases.

Some people see the glass half full; I see a little crack in the glass where stuff is slowly leaking out.

Know what you want to do. Know what you are able to do.

# 3
# WRITE FOR YOUR PRODUCER

Screenwriter and director Paul Schrader once said,

> I could be just a writer very easily. I am not a writer. I am a
> screenwriter, which is half a filmmaker . . . . But it is not an art
> form, because screenplays are not works of art. They are invita-
> tions to others to collaborate on a work of art.

Just like sheet music is not music, it is a document that tells the
musicians what to play, the screenplay is an instruction manual for a
film that tells directors, directors of photography, actors, production
designers, costume designers, etc., what they need to do for their job
on the film.

I write for the producer as much as I write for the director or the
actor.

What that means is that I write and teach my students to write in
a very spare, conservative style that results in what I call very user-
friendly screenplays. But it also means that I have to keep scope and
scale in mind when I write. I probably should not edit myself like this
when I write and maybe it is not really editing but it is writing with
the parameters in mind, being aware of what this production is and is
not going to be able to produce.

DOI: 10.4324/9781003138969-4

Alex Ross Perry told me:

> Part of being a writer on a micro-budget movie, for me was always also writing as a producer, because I can't, as a writer, write a movie that is going to be made where I've already told everybody, we're making it in July. And I've already basically gotten a sense of how much or how little money I'm going to have. As a writer, I cannot put in front of the producer an element in the script that is unachievable. And since I'm the only person wearing both of those hats, it is very easy for me to constantly be calibrating the script. Because the producer who knows how much money we're going to have is also sitting there writing the script.

My philosophy is that the screenplay is the instruction manual or blueprint for a film, and while it, of course, demands a high degree of artistry, the screenplay itself is not a work of art unto itself, it is the foundation of a film—a jumping-off place for directors, actors, cinematographers, etc., and so, at the most basic level, it has to be a working document that serves everyone on the crew, not weighed down by verbosity, literary conventions and flowery prose.

Now, I have heard from students who interned at production companies in L.A. and they tell me that some producers like flowery prose. Their philosophy is that flowery prose in a screenplay means that the author is a good writer. I do not subscribe to this philosophy.

Going in almost the opposite direction, I was judging screenplays for the Set in Philadelphia Screenwriting Competition for a few years and I came upon a screenplay that was almost the antithesis of what I teach. The screenplay was full of sentence fragments and editorial comments like "This woman will stop at nothing" that I usually scoff at. I was reading the screenplay and thinking to myself "What, this is not how to write a screenplay? Where did these people learn to write" but also, most importantly, "Why do I love this screenplay so much?" I finished reading it, filled out the review form and, when asked, I wrote emphatically that yes, this screenplay deserves to win. It won.

I was really rocked by the experience, wondering how a screen-play that was written in a style so opposite of the one I preach could be so effective. I reached out to a mentor and asked him for some thoughts because, most of the time, I am teaching "Introduction to Screenwriting" and I feel like students should learn the basics first, before they start getting into fancy stylistic flourishes and he agreed but tempered it with

> Ultimately, sentence fragments are perfectly acceptable, as long as the result is clarity. If you're conveying what we're supposed to see and, more important, what we're supposed to feel, the actual grammar isn't that important. If it helps the read without getting in the way of the read, it's okay, just don't show off.

And he went on to say that, at this point, I could probably stand to jazz up my writing style.

It's fun to come up with cool ideas and great scenes that will look good onscreen but be aware that these scenes will have to be produced and, if you are not also acting as the producer of this film, someone else will have to handle the logistics of shooting these scenes.

A few years ago, I was on a LinkedIn message board for producers. One of them posted the question "Producers, what is the hardest thing about working with screenwriters?" Many of the answers came down in the area of

> Most screenwriters have no idea about what actually goes into the nuts and bolts of day-to-day filmmaking; they just write stuff and expect us to be able to produce it without having any sense of the manpower, time and money involved.

Tom Quinn's first feature The New Year Parade (2008) won the Grand Jury Prize at Slamdance and his latest film Colewell (2019) was nominated for a couple of Independent Spirit Awards said,

> I think I don't know how to separate the writing and production, because I think they're not that separate. But I know for me, in the writing process, it's where I can explore things, make mistakes,

and not be spending money. But at least I can try a bunch of different things. And I was kind of surprised that when a friend asked to see The New Year Parade script at one point, I hadn't read in a long time and I was surprised by how close it was. Because in my mind, we just threw out the scripts, you know, the specifics of like, where things happen, during production.

Screenwriter Angela Marie Hutchinson has a degree in engineering but still needed a hand when it came time to reverse engineer her screenplay Hollywood Chaos (2013). Originally breaking into the film industry as a casting agent, she eventually started writing and producing.

I did not write with a low budget in mind for Hollywood Chaos. I actually wrote it as a $3,000,000 million movie. So definitely lower, not a huge budget. But I had actually tried to produce it before and it just never really panned out, like trying to raise the money, it was difficult, it was just difficult. So after doing casting on a couple of different movies as a casting director, I'd done maybe about six or seven independent movies, and I wasn't often on set and seeing how they did things, how everything was shot and how they kept the budget down, I was like, you know, I could probably try to do this again thinking of it as much, much cheaper. So then I just went forth with trying to raise the money and everything. Then once I had the money in place and we knew what we had to work with, I went back into the script and said, "Okay, my character is a basketball player. So instead of him playing with a whole stadium, we're going to have it be the offseason. So he's being interviewed, and he's just shooting hoops or working out or whatever it might be that just shows that he is a basketball player." So, yeah, I definitely feel that after I realized what our budget was, and was like, "Okay, the same (screenplay) is not possible. So how can we still do this?" But I didn't write with that in mind. I did end up working with a consultant to kind of bounce ideas off from a story perspective. We walked through some of the things to make sure from a story perspective, it wasn't being compromised, if we were changing this event, and just to look at it as a whole picture as opposed to like, just picking apart parts of the script that we had to pick apart for budget purposes. I went to the consultants and made sure that "Okay, here was our original script." And this is where we are now, does it still make sense? I see myself really, as a writer, fundamentally, I became a producer because I had to, I didn't ever think I wanted to produce movies. It was like, "I know, I want to write movies." And so they're like, "Oh, you have to produce them if you want them made." Okay, guess that's how it works.

I'm not saying that every screenwriter should know how to set up a C-stand or mic a scene in the woods, but being completely divorced from the production element of filmmaking can be a real disservice when it comes to writing for micro-budget. Say you put yourself out there as a screenwriter, you capture the attention of a producer or director with a little bit of money and they hire you to write a screenplay for a $50,000 film? You have to know what you can and cannot do in your screenplay and have a sense of what this group will be able to do on a meager budget.

Writer-director Bob Byington said,

> I think in some ways, if you're writing a script, it's helpful not to be thinking about the production and logistics and then in other ways it is. I really think that if I were a young person, or if I were trying to make a movie for no money, I would definitely be thinking about that at the writing stage. And you'd have to be a lunatic not to be thinking about it. If you're an established, skilled screenwriter, no, I don't think you should be thinking about the budget. But if you're, if you're a kid, or if you're going to make a movie and you have $65,000, then you should have your head examined for not thinking about the logistics.

So, while it is not going to suit every writer or every production, if possible, I recommend that screenwriters spend at least a little time on a set or, if nothing else, in a production meeting so that they can hear what producers, AD's, UPM's and so on discuss.

Filmmaking is a team sport and the screenplay, while critically important to the success of the film, is only one element of the collaborative process. It is not enough for me to be happy with the screenplay: everyone else involved with the film has to like it too. It takes a variety of people doing different things together to make it happen, but, honestly, I didn't think the teamwork element applied to the screenplay.

When I was just starting out, I naively thought that the process would be "I write the screenplay and the team makes it" but came to realize that there has to be a degree of teamwork in the writing stage. I have to be open to input, questions, suggestions and different perspectives because, at this point, I am usually not the person who is making the film.

The person who is making the film either asked me to write a screenplay based on his/her ideas or saw something in one of my original screenplays that he/she wanted to produce. It becomes my job to serve the producer or director's vision even if I was the one who came up with the idea in the first place. Ultimately, at some stage in the process, I have to sign off on the screenplay, walk away from it, let the production team do whatever they want to it—while I cower in the shadows and hope for the best.

The L.A. producer who optioned Stomping Ground in 2009 wanted me to make a number of changes to it in the six months that we worked together. The development and re-writing process was the hardest work as a writer that I have ever been asked to do. Honestly, I have often been able to coast on the relative strength of generally decent work but relative strength and general decency were not going to cut it in L.A. and I was really stretched and challenged. The result was a screenplay that is much deeper and richer, more solid than I could have done on my own.

Oh, yes, you might think that you sell a screenplay and that's the end, but, no, you can be kept in limbo doing rewrite after rewrite. In my case, the producer who optioned it optioned an 80-page screenplay and, by the time I made all of the requested changes, it had ballooned up to 104 pages before gradually coming back down to 98, 96, 92, 86 and, finally 82 pages! She told me to make all of these changes and then we whittled it all down until it was nearly identical to the original screenplay, but this process had somehow made it much stronger, as if all of the stuff we added and then took out left some kind of narrative residue behind.

This is just something to consider because writing a screenplay is only part of the battle, and getting someone to produce it and then someone else to distribute it are massive mountains to climb and the further and further you try to climb, the less and less control you have. I have seen too many micro-budget films not make it all the way up the mountain.

Writer-director Martha Stephens said "I think I still have that mindset when I'm writing where I am writing practically. Because even though I might be writing something with a bigger budget, I'm still thinking like, 'how is this going to get made?'"

I often tell my film students that it can be as hard to make a bad movie as it is to make a good movie.

I remember watching a terrible movie on DVD a few years ago, then watching the "making of" special feature and seeing how much time, mental and physical effort went into the production of this awful film, how earnest and hardworking they were, etc.—I guess the disconnect is at the point where someone or some people all missed the fact that the screenplay was bad and went forward with millions and millions of dollars to sail this doomed voyage.

On a film crew, everyone thinks that their job is the most important. Directors often think they are the most important person on set. Actors often think they are the most important person on set. I once worked with a gaffer who clearly thought he was the most important person on set. But, for me, as the screenwriter who might not even be on set, I know that my job really is pretty darn important because, without me, nobody else has a job to do, right?

Back when I reviewed films for IndieTalk, I criticized the filmmakers of a film I had to watch for having a terrible screenplay, but I wrote that I didn't mean to single them out, that bad screenplays are a real issue in many of the films that I review for this site.

So, what is the problem? Okay, I know that I am going to get a lot of grief for this next statement, but, as a screenwriting professor, it often seems to me that many students go to film school to learn how to push buttons on machines.

Yes, film is a mechanical art; it utilizes technology and cinematographers, editors, audio engineers and visual effects; artists need to know how to use these tools. Screenwriting is a class that all film students have to take and many of them are not especially interested in it, they are just looking to fulfill the requirement. I get it, some people are intimidated by writing or insecure about their writing and screenwriting involves learning about story structure, formula and formatting, all of which might be off-putting to budding cinematographers and editors.

It is hard to come up with ideas for film and there are no machines out there and no buttons to push to make it happen on its own. Yes, without taking a deep dive into the topic, there are AI screenwriting programs out there and, to be completely honest, from the little I have seen, they seem to do a surprisingly good job. I suspect that there are working screenwriters out there who secretly use these tools.

Too many of "us" in the indie world seem to be too focused on technology, so much so that the foundation of a film is being ignored. I implore you, the film community, to put your camera down, stop tapping your keyboard and invest in what I consider essential filmmaking equipment: a good book or two on screenwriting.

For $20 or less, you can buy a book that will open your eyes to the magic of plotting out a story, usually in accordance with the Three-Act Structure. I know that a lot of technical, creative people are intimidated by screenwriting that they find it mysterious and daunting to have to learn "the formula" and the formatting but it really helps.

I already mentioned that screenwriters who do not have a firm grasp on what takes place in production will be doing themselves and their collaborators a big service if they educate themselves about production. Your producers will thank you for it. Read your screenplay the way a producer reads a screenplay. Yes, of course, they have to like your story, but they also have to figure out if and how to make it.

Even if you just learn the basics, it can make your films and your approach to filmmaking so much better and I will not have to sit through films where the inciting incident comes 45 minutes into the story—okay, yes, I know that the inciting incident in The Godfather (1972) comes around an hour into it but it is not the early 1970s; you are probably not Francis Ford Coppola and that kind of move is pretty hard to pull off. Learn the basic concepts of structure, conflicts, what makes a strong main character, etc., and it might be revolutionary to you.

So, I hate to sound cranky, but I am seeing a lot of low-budget indie films made by people who know how to shoot well, light well, edit well, do special effects well but cannot tell an interesting, compelling story and that should not be the case. It is really not that hard to come up with a story for a film. Yes, it is hard to come up with an original, intelligent story for a film, but so many people are just aiming to make basic, ordinary films anyway and there is nothing wrong with that IF the story is strong, the structure is sound and the characters are compelling.

Noam Kroll said,

> From a production level, filmmakers often do try to, I guess they feel the biggest challenge is that they want their movie to look like a "real movie." They want it to feel like a real movie, but, when you're competing in the same sort of territory or arena as these other films that have way more money and way more resources and producers attached and stars attached, you're never going to win at that game because they've beat you before you even start. So try to create your own game that they can't compete with because their system is going to have more of a hierarchy. It's going to have more of a chain of command and a lot more cooks in the kitchen. And, when you're working on that level, that can be incredibly frustrating. So why not? There's no need to sort of try to emulate that when you have a lot more freedom in the early days making these smaller films.

He continued,

> I knew from the get go, we would only be filming in two locations. Other than a couple of shots, everything was either one house or the other house, and we only have four to five days depending on the home to shoot in. And obviously that's not a lot of time for a feature film. We had to fly through these scenes. When I was writing the script, I tried to make sure that none of the scenes with a couple of exceptions were longer than two pages. In some cases I wanted everything to be like one page or page and a half. And that was sort of a rule that I imposed on myself right away, because I knew when it did get into production, it would get complicated to cover those scenes. Let's say there was a five or six page dialogue scene, things would get more complicated because we couldn't just shoot it as a one or it would get boring, that the visual is not interesting. So with this, by keeping the scenes short, I basically knew, okay, no matter what, we can, if we had to, we could shoot every scene in this movie just from one angle. So if we're reaching the end of the day and you know, we're losing time and we had to do it all in a one, it would be possible because we're just shooting these quick little scenes. And from a writing perspective, it helped to keep things fresh too, because I think when you give yourself all the time in the world to write a scene, you don't always get to the heart or the meat of what it is for a while. There could be a lot of dialogue back and forth, a lot of wasted space on the page. And you end up trimming that down anyways, whether it's on set or in the editing room. So by forcing this one to two page per scene format onto the screenplay, it made me do a lot of the editing work as I was writing, because I was just immediately just saying, "Okay, if this doesn't fit, or if this isn't a hundred percent necessary, just lose it."

So, by all means, while you are waiting for your Blackmagic to arrive, pick up a good book on screenwriting, learn the basics and apply them to your next film, please.

# 4

# SCREENWRITING HACKS

Writing a screenplay for a low-budget film is not like writing a screenplay for big-budget films. There will usually be fewer characters, fewer locations and fewer scenes. The scenes are often much longer than scenes in films with big budgets. There is a real danger of scenes becoming static and stagy.

Your story has to account for audience fatigue, the fact that they might get tired of looking at the same scenery after a while. Build drama into your story at regular intervals, employ locations within locations (sub-locations), incorporate motion as much as possible and have characters doing things, not just sitting around.

To me, screenwriting involves two distinct phases, the Creative Conceptual Phase and the Creative Mechanical Phase.

The Creative Conceptual Phase is where you formulate your characters, plot, themes and figure out the way your film is going to unfold. In a micro-budget film, the Creative Conceptual Phase is where to figure out what you are going to be capable of doing in your film and how to plan for it in the story.

I am a big fan of outlining. It took me a while to embrace outlining. If you think about it, many people prefer to get right into the writing. Outlining forces us to think everything through before jumping into the project. For me, it is a great way to organize all of my thoughts before I start to write and I would

DOI: 10.4324/9781003138969-5

rather be organized when writing than making things up as I go along.

If you were going somewhere for the first time, would you look up the address, put it into GPS and then figure out the best way to get there or would you just hit the road and hope for the best? To me, outlining is narrative GPS.

If you have a strong outline, moving into the Creative Mechanical Phase will be much smoother. The Creative Mechanical Phase is where you are actually writing the screenplay. Of course, it involves a lot of creativity because your time should be spent focusing on writing rich but efficient scene descriptions and dialogue. Ideally, you should be focused on writing scene descriptions and dialogue, not story. To me, you should not be working out story issues while writing scene descriptions and dialogue, the story should have been worked out before starting to write the screenplay so that you can place your energy on the Creative Mechanical elements of the screenplay.

I got hired to write a screenplay once and the producer said "Great, I will send over the outline." He sent over a rich, complete ten-page outline. Boom, I could get right down to the writing. Another time, the same thing happened and, when I opened the outline, all I saw was one paragraph. I could not get right down to the writing because the story was not completely there. I had to write big chunks of the story and fill in lots of blanks, not what I was expecting to do.

There are countless ways to write an outline. If you search "How To Write An Outline," you will find an overwhelming number of philosophies and approaches. Do not get overwhelmed, do what feels right to you. Just get your ideas out of your head and into a document. The outline should be a really personal document that represents your creative work style and serves to inspire you in the Creative Mechanical Phase. Some people write outlines that are basically screenplays without dialogue. That works. Some people include artwork and music in their outline. Some outlines read like journal entries. I call outlining the Creative Conceptual Phase because there is so much thinking involved before you even start to write. There is that saying about writers never taking a vacation because they are always either writing or thinking about writing.

So, when I am finally feeling ready to start outlining, I open a new document and begin to type in random thoughts for characters, scenes, lines of dialogue, locations, themes, references to other films and so on. Once I have seven to ten pages of these notes, I stare at them deeply and get a feel for where they would fit into the story. Then I start cutting and pasting the notes into some sort of rough beginning, middle and end order. Once the notes start to feel like they are in order, I expand upon them, fill in details and then start to come up with the narrative connective tissue that will bind everything into a coherent story.

When I feel that this process is successful, I will usually have a seven- to ten-page outline that I keep open on my desktop as I write the screenplay. I write a scene and then refer to the outline to see what scene comes next. To me, if I write a scene and then have to ask myself "What should happen now?" I have not done an effective job of writing an outline. That question should have been answered in the Creative Mechanical Phase.

When I teach outlining in my classes, I always tell students

> Because of the current dynamic where I am the professor and you are in my class, I have to give you a grade on your outline but the true grade will come from you because, if the process of writing your screenplay is smooth, it is because you wrote a good outline and if it is rocky, chances are good that your outline could have used more work. Only you will know if you did a good job on the outline.

Now, this method works for me and I think you cannot go wrong with it, but that does not mean there are other approaches.

We have touched on the topic of taking stock of your resources, figuring out what assets you already have in place that can be utilized in your film. Next, it is time to figure out how best to stretch those resources. Of course, as mentioned here and there, your film is probably going to have limited characters and locations.

A film with limited characters and locations? That sounds sort of like a play. There is a lot of sense to, at least, start thinking about your film as a play. Now is as good a time as any to mention one of the classics of low-budget filmmaking that embraced the concepts necessary to make this kind of film. Polly Schattel said, "The original conception of Reservoir Dogs (1992) was as a smaller $30,000 budget, indie film with just like five characters, almost like a play."

Lawrence Michael Levine talked about thinking about writing as if for a play when he took classes with Tom Noonan.

> I learned so much from Tom Noonan. I studied with him for about three and a half years. He didn't really teach any kind of traditional storytelling stuff, Three-Act Structure or eight sequence structure or anything like that, it was really a great way to learn dialogue writing. And he had an interesting setup where he taught writing and acting. And in the writing class, what he would do is he would bring in actors from the acting class to read your material. And for me, there was no real issue between theater and film. Cassavetes did plenty of work in the theater. I was looking at stuff like My Dinner With Andre (1981). The Harold Pinter stuff that the BBC did, all this kind of stuff.
>
> So a couple of people from Tom's class started a theatre company. And they were looking for work. And I just decided, "Okay, well, these guys have a theatre company. They're my friends. Maybe they'll put up my play." So I started to work on a full length and showed it to them, and then they put it up. And, I was encouraged by the reaction to it. So, for me, the natural thing was just like, "Okay, well, I want to turn this into a film." What I really wanted to do is make films, I just didn't have the possibility. And it was sort of like, 'Wow, that play was coming out.' The DV cams were coming out. And I was like, "Okay, so now you can just make a movie on this video."

That looks pretty good when it's blown up. So I'm going to do that. And so we cobbled together some money, the people who produced the play, helped me out, and I think paid for half of it. So I think it was just like 10 grand, and from them and 10 grand from my dad. Yeah, and, and we made a movie of Territory (2005). So that was my first experience of film-making. I was actually enrolled at film school, right after my play had come out. So I shot it over Christmas break of my first year of school.

There is only so much you can do onstage. Yes, there have been big-budget Broadway productions where characters fly or there is rain onstage, but, much like a micro-budget film, when trying to mount a play on a modest budget, there is only so much you can do onstage.

Scenes tend to be longer onstage mostly because set changes can be complicated. In film, long scenes are usually not as natural. As recently as the 1990s, the average movie scene was two or three minutes long and today, the average scene is about ninety seconds long. I know that, in my process of writing non-micro-budget films, if I find a scene stretching past three pages, I am already starting to look for a way out, already telling myself that something might not be working.

So, in a micro-budget film with limited locations—i.e., set changes—there is, by nature, an increased chance of having longer scenes. The trick is to find ways to keep these scenes from becoming too static or stagy. Sure, one way is to make these scenes extra dramatic, comedic or otherwise active narratively, but that is not going to be possible in every scene.

The easiest, perhaps most obvious, hack might not always be available but will likely be available more times than not. Simply breaking scenes up into sub-scenes where, instead of having two people sit on the couch and talk for eight minutes, have them get up, go to the kitchen for two minutes, maybe go back to the couch for a couple minutes and maybe go into another room for two minutes. The dialogue doesn't have to change.

Here is an example from a screenplay I wrote a few years ago. To put it in context, it is about a teenage boy, Ryan, who discovers that his boring accountant father, Julius, had once been the lead guitarist of a briefly semi-famous 1980s hair metal band, Iron Teardrop (because who doesn't like any opportunity to come up with a band name?):

> *For context: teenage Ryan and his father, Julius are estranged following a divorce. Ryan does not think much of his boring, basic father until he discovers his dark secret, that, in the 80's, Julius was Maxx Voluume, guitarist for the briefly famous hair metal band Iron Teardrop. In this scene, Ryan reveals that he knows the truth about Julius by showing him a replica of a guitar made sort of famous in a music video.*

VERSION I:

INT. JULIUS'S APARTMENT—DAY
Julius and Ryan sit at the table. Ryan glances at him anxiously then opens the guitar case to reveal Julius' guitar from the video.
They glance at each other knowingly.

RYAN: I got it on eBay.
JULIUS: E-bay. I mean, this thing must have cost . . .
Beat.
RYAN: Not really.
JULIUS: No, probably not.
RYAN: I told the seller I was your son.
Julius picks up the guitar awkwardly.
RYAN (CONT'D): How come you never told me?
JULIUS: How did you find out?
RYAN: Hannah was looking for . . .
JULIUS: For?
RYAN: Costumes for a party . . .
JULIUS: Pretty funny wasn't it?

Ryan's eyes widen as Julius adopts his old 80's persona.

JULIUS (CONT'D): Didn't know your old man used to be Maxx Voluume?

RYAN: So . . .

JULIUS: So, why didn't I tell you? I think you already have your answer.

RYAN: I do?

Julius hands the guitar to Ryan.

JULIUS: You guys were looking for a costume, right, something to parody, laugh at, make fun of . . .

RYAN: Dad, I mean, it's not like that.

JULIUS: It is, Ryan. Always has been. It was joke, a joke from the start, a joke that everyone but the band got.

RYAN: What do you mean?

JULIUS: I loved music. I played everything, all the time. That wasn't what I wanted to do, what I wanted to be. I didn't get into it to be laughed at.

RYAN: But . . .

JULIUS: It just happened and, before I knew it, I was making money, money I made by, I don't know, selling my soul. I'm embarrassed by it.

RYAN: But the people, everyone who bought your albums and went to your shows . . .

JULIUS: What about them?

RYAN: You think they're embarrassed? Okay, maybe now, maybe a little but, back then . . .

JULIUS: Back then?

RYAN: It kinda looks like they were all having a good time . . . . You made people happy, dad. No, maybe you didn't change lives or inspire a generation but, I don't know, being able to say that, for awhile, you were part of something that took people out of their everyday lives for a bit, made them happy for a minute . . . That's kinda cool, isn't it?

Julius, chokes up, looks over at Ryan.

RYAN (CONT'D): Well, I know you said you have something to do . . .

JULIUS: Yeah, I really should be going . . .

They eye each other expectantly.

VERSION II:

### INT. JULIUS'S APARTMENT—DAY

Julius and Ryan sit at the table. Ryan glances at him anxiously then opens the guitar case to reveal Julius' guitar from the video.

They glance at each other knowingly.

RYAN: I got it on eBay.

JULIUS: E-bay. I mean, this thing must have cost . . .

Beat.

RYAN: Not really.

JULIUS: No, probably not.

RYAN: I told the seller I was your son.

Julius picks up the guitar awkwardly.

RYAN (CONT'D): How come you never told me?

JULIUS: How did you find out?

RYAN: Hannah was looking for . . .

JULIUS: For?

RYAN: Costumes for a party . . .

JULIUS: Pretty funny wasn't it?

Ryan's eyes widen as Julius adopts his old 80's persona.

JULIUS (CONT'D): Didn't know your old man used to be Maxx Voluume?

RYAN: So . . .

JULIUS: So, why didn't I tell you? I think you already have your answer.

RYAN: I do?

Julius heads into the kitchen.

### INT. JULIUS'S KITCHEN—DAY

Ryan enters the kitchen with the guitar and hands it back to Julius.

JULIUS: You guys were looking for a costume, right, something to parody, laugh at, make fun of.

RYAN: Dad, I mean, it's not like that.

JULIUS: It is, Ryan. Always has been. It was joke, a joke from the start, a joke that everyone but the band got.

RYAN: What do you mean?

JULIUS: I loved music. I played everything, all the time. That wasn't what I wanted to do, what I wanted to be.

(MORE)

JULIUS (CONT'D):   I didn't get into it to be laughed at.

Julius strums the guitar absently but expertly.

RYAN:   But . . .

JULIUS:   It just happened and, before I knew it, I was making money, money I made by, I don't know, selling my soul. I'm embarrassed by it.

He hands the guitar back to Ryan and heads into the living room.

INT. JULIUS'S APARTMENT—DAY

Ryan follows Julius in.

RYAN:   But the people, everyone who bought your albums and went to your shows . . .

JULIUS:   What about them?

RYAN:   You think they're embarrassed? Okay, maybe now, maybe a little but, back then . . .

JULIUS:   Back then?

RYAN:   It kinda looks like they were all having a good time . . . . You made people happy, dad. No, maybe you didn't change lives or inspire a generation but, I don't know, being able to say that, for awhile, you were part of something that took people out of their everyday lives for a bit, made them happy for a minute . . . That's kinda cool, isn't it?

Julius, chokes up, looks over at Ryan.

RYAN (CONT'D):   Well, I know you said you have something to do . . .

JULIUS:   Yeah, I really should be going . . .

They eye each other expectantly. Ryan hands the guitar to Julius.

Nothing fancy, nothing radical, no lines change, but the scene is more active and dynamic visually because of the diversion into the kitchen and the addition of "symbolic gestures" with the guitar.

Now, importantly, while breaking scenes up in this manner will keep the final product a little more lively, in production, it will add another set-up. Instead of just knocking out three or four pages in the living room, you will have to shoot the scene on that set, break down the lights and camera and then move everything to the kitchen. So, you might not want to do this kind of thing in every scene, but, if you are worried about having too many talky scenes in your screen-play, breaking scenes up can be a helpful hack.

This approach came up with Noam Kroll, who said:

> How are you going to keep those scenes interesting and keep the camera moving or keep the angles changing? So sometimes what I would do if I had a scene that I felt like it should've been five pages or six pages and it was all gonna take place in one room. I might just break it up and split it in thirds, and I'd have the first third of the scene take place in this room. I did this little transition experiment; we did these little black frames to transition from scene to scene. And then, when it would come back, then we would jump ahead, be in a differ-ent location and we sort of pick up the conversation or we'd pick up some of the details. So, by doing that, essentially, I had my same five or six page scene, but it just became three smaller scenes, which in this case just made practical sense. Some peo-ple liked it and the other people didn't, but that was kind of part of the fun.

He continued,

> So, in the script itself, while I didn't do any camera direction or anything like that, I did try to infuse a lot of visual language into the scene descriptions in a way that would at least give me and hopefully, the actors and the other crew members, the con-fidence as they're reading the script that there was going to be some sort of progression in every scene that it wasn't just, these characters are talking in a room.

But again, I think that's where the scene descriptions came into play. And I think if you can create that feeling on the page where things are changing and progressing and where you get a sense that from scene to scene, the tone is shifting and the mood is shifting. Even though I wasn't using camera direction, you could kind of picture that. And "Sure, we've been in the living room before, but we've only seen it during the day. So now we're seeing it at night. So it's going to kind of feel like a different environment. So I think it's all about like, you know, it really does come down to just embracing those limitations and while you're writing, looking for just some sort of measure of progression."

Another way to break up scenes is with flashbacks. Now, in my circle, I have gained a reputation for being militantly anti-flashbacks. The charge is partly true. It is just that, too often, I see flashbacks (and for that matter, voiceovers) used to fill in plot holes rather than as an integral part of the storytelling style. Double Indemnity (1944) is a beloved classic, cited by a number of directors as one of their favorite films. The film is almost entirely flashbacks and voice-overs that completely work to make a great film. Speaking of beloved classics, I know I am alone here, but I feel that Casablanca (1942) would have been fine without the single flashback in it. Does the flashback provide the specifics of exactly what happened between Rick and Ilsa? Sure. Did it tell me anything I needed to know that I did not already know? Ilsa is Rick's ex-girlfriend and I knew that without the flashback. Deadpool (2016) effectively used an escalating series of flashbacks to show how the character arrived at his current state.

Dead Funny (1994) is a not widely known film but remains a personal favorite of mine from the mid-90s indie era. It's not available on DVD or on streaming services, but, at the risk of coming off as a fanboy, I contacted John Feldman, the director, and he made a copy for me. While technically not a micro-budget film in the context of this book, it clearly exemplifies many of the concepts discussed here and it was inspiring to me in those earlier days as a beginning screenwriter. The bulk of the film is set in one apartment and gets around the potential for staginess by not just employing flashbacks; it employs flashbacks within flashbacks that all take place in the apartment.

Another hack that will only be appropriate in certain cases is musical performances. Of course, a micro-budget musical is a tall order, but it has been done. Before Whiplash and LA LA Land, Damian

Chazelle made the black and white, 72-minute-long musical Guy and Madeline on a Park Bench (2009) for a reported $60,000. While a little bit over the $100,000 figure used as the baseline for this book, Once (2007) is another example worth looking at. Honestly, I have never been able to get my hands on the screenplay. I even asked at the WGA library and they had a digital copy, but, as I was there at the very beginning of the 2020 pandemic, they were not allowing anyone to access their iPads. At 86 minutes long, it contains performances of complete songs, which leads me to wonder if the action and dialogue portions of the screenplay were in the 50–60 page range. Conveniently, I did have an opportunity to write a musical that never got produced but my screenplay was, in fact, 43 pages long and indicated spaces for several complete performances of songs.

Next, while more of a production concern, a producer I worked with when she optioned a screenplay of mine suggested that I have as many two-person scenes as possible. The reasoning is that, once you add additional characters to a scene, you are dramatically increasing the amount of coverage that needs to be shot.

A hack that you can build into your screenplay via dialogue is creating a vivid outside world for your characters. Create images in the minds of audiences; describe people, places and events in provocative detail. After a screening of Stomping Ground, someone came up to me and said:

> Don't take this the wrong way but watching the film was sort of like listening to an audiobook because the characters reference all of these different places and people we never see on screen so we are forced to create images in our heads.

I took it as a compliment. You never see the antagonist in the film, but you hear so much about him that it is hard not to form an image of him in your mind.

The first scene of Reservoir Dogs is a model of an effectively dynamic one-location scene. At around ten minutes long, the scene is full of snappy dialogue aided by some flashy camerawork and editing, but what it does so well is pique the attention of the audience, who is left wondering "What is going on here?" What it does especially well is establish a tone that is then radically subverted in the first scene after the opening credits. It has been done before and I am not sure if it will ever be done quite as well, but the rest of us can give it a shot—without borrowing too heavily from it.

Not exactly a hack in the conventional sense but it is important to keep in mind that good stories come from good characters. Okay, that advice applies to screenwriting in general, but it is especially important on a micro-budget film where you are unlikely to distract the audience with stunts, special effects and exotic locations. Face it, the audience is going to be spending a lot of time getting to know your characters and, if much of what they are doing on screen involves talking, they better be interesting people in a captivating situation. I think an actor's face is the greatest special effect we have at our disposal in general but especially at this level. Torture your characters, put them through hell and, by doing so, you are giving your actors a lot to work with.

Depending on your perspective, creating a character is your opportunity to play either God or Dr. Frankenstein. Unlike actually parenting a real person who will grow up and develop their own personality based on environmental factors and nurturing, you are inventing someone: their background, strengths, weaknesses, wants, wishes and desires as well as the internal and external obstacles that sometimes interfere with the pursuit of their goals.

You create a character who has challenges and then throw your character into situations that put them to the test. If your character is not being tested, pushed to their limits and beyond, there is a good chance that your screenplay is not as effective as it could be.

Now, this is just me and my process, but I need to know what kind of music my character listens to. For me, if I don't know what kind of music my character listens to, I don't know my character and, if I don't know my character, I don't know my story.

Remember, as if you can forget, that we are talking about film, not narrative prose here. It's been said that a novelist has to be the writer, director, cinematographer, costume designer, set builder and so on when writing a book. In film, if we want to show something, we put it in front of a camera. The human brain is designed to take in, then analyze data and make a decision about it, so, when your characters first appear on screen, the audience will make assumptions about who they are. Remember the phrase "don't judge a book by its cover"? It means do not prejudge. In film, we want the audience to prejudge, we want them to know or at least think they know who the character "is" when they first see them. It is the screenwriter's job to design book covers for the filmmakers to produce.

While we get to know and invest in a character over the course of a film, it is important to establish your character as soon as they appear in your film. John August, one of the few people out there who is both a successful screenwriter and a well-respected speaker, writer, blogger and podcaster on the subject of screenwriting said, when asked how quickly he knows that he is reading a screenplay that is not working "To me, it's as the first few characters are introduced. If character introductions are not done artfully, the odds of anything else in the script being great are slim."

Harsh maybe but pretty accurate. I love teaching students about character introductions, but there is just not enough room in this book for a deep dive into the subject. Just think about it when you are writing. Imagine the way your character appears for the first time in your film. People, in general, judge books by their covers and they do it every day; it's called prejudice in some places and street smarts in others. Think about it, have you ever seen someone walking down the street and thought "He looks like a dick. He looks like he could use a slap in the face." One of my favorite examples of a character arc in visuals is the opening and closing of Saturday Night Fever (1977). When we first meet Tony Manero, in the opening credits of the film, before he even says a word, he is strutting down the street in a black leather jacket, acting like he thinks he is all that. He looks like he could use a slap in the face. In the final scenes of the film, he is wearing a white jacket, has been taken down a notch or two and has a bandage on his face.

No need to answer me. Put this concept to work in your story. How do you engineer a character introduction that establishes the desired first impression of your character? The audience should know or, at least, make a snap judgment about your characters before they even say a word. People say a lot with fashion style, grooming, demeanor and what they are doing. I still remember working on a film school project in Philadelphia's Rittenhouse Square and seeing a heavyset man walking through the park, smoking a cigarette and wearing a t-shirt with an image of a barbell and the words "Workin' Out" above it. That image made an impression. I made assumptions and a judgment about this guy. You want the audience to make assumptions and judgments about your characters. Bottom line: when a character appears onscreen for the first time, we take in the data, analyze it and make a decision about how we feel about them.

In the film Non-Stop (2014), the first time we see Liam Neeson, it is morning, he parks his car at the airport, opens his glove box, takes out a bottle and does three shots. How do you feel about a guy who does three shots first thing in the morning before getting on a plane? There's got to be a story there, right? Next, as he is entering the airport, a guy approaches him and asks for a cigarette. At that moment, I said to myself "Okay, he's going to be the bad guy." For the next 87 minutes or so, the movie bends over backward to suggest that any number of other characters are the bad guy(s) but, in the end, yup, SPOILER ALERT—it was that first guy. Now, truth be told, the same thing happened to me when I saw Taken. A big chunk of the first ten minutes is spent establishing Neeson's card-playing buddies, so I naturally assumed that one or some of them were setting him up. Wrong. These well-established characters never appear again.

So, when conceiving of your micro-budget screenplay, always keep in mind any narrative/visual shortcuts that can keep costs down.

I spoke with writer-director Vera Brunner-Sung about her remarkable feature Bella Vista (2014), asked about engineering hacks into a screenplay for a micro-budget film and she gave me a wonderfully candid answer.

DG: Did you engineer any, in any specific hacks or anything, presuming that you were going to go with an ultra low budget? Did you write specifically for that?

VBS: I mean, I guess, I guess, but, you know, I feel like this question presumes some kind of knowledge about how much a movie is supposed to be. I just didn't really have a sense of how to budget it until I got my producers on board. But, in my mind, the mantra was just like, "simple."

# 5

# STORY STRUCTURE

I am sure that someone else has said what I am about to say, but I cannot find it anywhere or attribute to anyone so, for now, I am calling it Greenberg's Formula:

Screenplay = Idea + Story + Plot

Idea—The overall premise, themes and thoughts that inform the film.
Story—Everything that happens either onscreen or off even before the movie starts.
Plot—Everything that happens on screen.

Note that this approach does not prescribe page numbers where major beats should occur; it is a general overview of how a story can unfold.

A simplified example:

Spielberg says, "I know, I have an Idea that I would like to express—'War is bad'"

So there is this Story about the four Ryan brothers who go off to fight in World War II. Three of them are killed, and the Army decides to find the other one and bring him back alive to avoid a public relations nightmare.

The Plot then follows Tom Hanks and a band of broadly drawn characters as they hunt for Private Ryan, many of them getting killed

DOI: 10.4324/9781003138969-6

along the way and leading the audience to realize how Bad War Is and how brutal WWII was. The three dead Ryan brothers are part of the story but not part of the plot because, for the most part, their deaths occur offscreen before the start of the movie.

Make sense?

To be honest, my roots are in theater, offbeat, avant-garde or absurdist theater. I have been influenced by more playwrights (Pinter, Albee, Stoppard and Ionesco) and stand-up comedians (Richard Pryor, Bill Cosby and Steve Martin) than I have been by screenwriters.

I gravitate toward the unconventional, so books like Syd Field's iconic Screenplay and Blake Syder's massively popular but wildly divisive Save The Cat, which have lots of useful material, are really geared toward conventional, commercial mainstream films. Alternative Screenwriting by Jeff Rush and Ken Dancyger is one of my favorite books—period, not just a favorite screenwriting book, a favorite book.

Yes, I had misgivings about including a quote from Woody Allen in Chapter 2. From the start, there was a filmmaker I planned to interview for this book, but, when charges of sexual assault made the news, I decided against it. Similarly, I am conflicted about discussing Bill Cosby and I hope you will forgive me.

In my teens, I dabbled in stand-up comedy and even dipped my toes into that pool now and then. My parents knew Bill Cosby in college. I listened to a lot of Cosby growing up.

In 1980, I went to see Bill Cosby at the York, PA State Fair. He came out and told one funny story, went off on a slightly related tangent, came back to the story, went off on another slightly related tangent, came back to the story and repeated the process for an hour.

It was one of the most brilliant, unified, cohesive pieces of stagecraft I have ever seen, so carefully plotted and conceived that I was truly left in awe.

The act had a narrative spine and everything else grew out of it organically, nothing was random and it all served to support the whole piece, the overall idea. A film should be about something and all the scenes should serve to make your overall point.

So, have you ever seen a bad movie? What was bad about it? Costume design? Sound effects editing? Or was it something like "I just don't buy that this character would have done that" or "it wasn't funny" or "it wasn't scary" or "it was stupid" or "it was too long." Even worse, have you ever seen a movie that started out well but fell apart later? Most of the time, it is rarely the cinematography, the editing, costume design, the DIT, craft services or special effects that is the issue; it is usually because the screenplay needed more work. Most of the time, if a movie is bad, it is because there were issues with the screenplay. Of course, let's not forget that, on the other hand, most of the time, if a movie is really good, it's usually because the screenplay was really good.

In certain circles like theater and TV, the writer and the script are considered an almost holy text that is not to be messed with. Of course, plays and TV shows are tweaked in production, but it is rarely ever like the assembly line approach to writing many major movies. The WGA allows only three screenwriters or screenwriting teams to be credited with the screenplay for a film, but it is not uncommon for dozens of uncredited writers to contribute to the final product.

So, how should you approach the screenplay for your micro-budget film? As mentioned earlier, this book assumes a degree of familiarity with the basic concepts of screenwriting. Maybe you have taken a class, read some books on the topic and studied screenplays for films you like. If you read enough screenwriting books, you might come to the conclusion that the Three-Act Structure rules.

Many of the filmmakers interviewed for this book had strong feelings about applying the Three-Act Structure in their films.

I spoke with director Ry Russo-Young about the approach to her earlier films Orphans (2007), You Won't Miss Me (2009) and Nobody Walks (2012).

DG: I want to go back to the conceptual phase of Orphans, and take stock of parameters, and things like that, which is a pretty classic model now that everyone knows.

RY RUSSO-YOUNG: Obviously, it's a highly charged situation, the scenario is already dramatic. And there's conflict and an emotional void before the movie even starts, I mean, so you're starting at a kind of an emotional high point.

DG: But then as a writer, when you're writing the script for this very, you know, limited location set story. How did you engineer in more conflict and crisis to the degree that you did?

RRY: I mean, just to keep the story going. Yeah, things escalate. But I guess that's screenwriting 101.

DG: But were you concerned about the dynamics of it manifesting in the one location?

Some people have applied conventional Three-Act Structure to their micro-budget films.

RRY: My personal feeling was always that you needed it even more, when you were in a contained space, again, needed to rely on those tenets of drama. And if you look at movies like Rope (1948) or something that have been made with very limited settings or even the Polanski film Repulsion (1965) or something like that, those are very much using the Three-Act Structure and are very, very creative, within a narrow confines in a box.

Do not get me wrong, I like plenty of conventional, commercial mainstream films, but that type of film can be hard to make on a micro-budget that has limited characters and locations; so, if you are short on funds, there is a good chance that you are looking at making an unconventional film that could struggle to find a mainstream audience and yield much commercial success. Embrace that status, look outside of the box and come up with the best idea for a film you can make with what you have access to.

As a screenwriting teacher and a writer for hire, I have found that I frequently have to utilize the Three-Act Structure. I have taught the Three-Act Structure in my Introduction to Screenwriting course over 100 times since 2004. I frequently refer to the Three-Act Structure as "screenwriting with training wheels." Most people learn to ride a bike by using training wheels. Few people just hop on a bike for the first time and compete in the Tour De France. Most screenwriters learn the "rules" of screenwriting before producing anything. So, the metaphor is appropriate. Take Advanced Screenwriting or

Screenplay Story Development with me and things are different. That said, I have come to recognize and appreciate Three-Act as a beautiful thing, a really effective model to hang a story on, a convention to work within, a formula to follow—yes, when we talk about films being formulaic, we are talking about the Three-Act Structure. I can appreciate when a film hits its marks like a precision instrument as much as I can appreciate the rare film that defies convention and still succeeds.

But to slavishly adhere to the formula is to intentionally rule out other approaches to your story and maybe to push the boundaries of convention that have the potential to render it fresh and original. Look at some recent Oscar-winning screenplays and ask yourself if they truly follow the Three-Act Structure in the conventional way—a sympathetic, needy protagonist is unwillingly thrown out of his/her comfort zone and forced to take action in order to achieve a goal, encountering obstacles and setbacks along the way that ultimately result in the protagonist growing and changing as a person for the better.

In 2010, screenplays based on true stories won the Oscars for the best original screenplay and best-adapted screenplay. In the first scene of The King's Speech, Bertie is second in line to the throne—he's unlikely to ever become king—and his profound speech impediment makes it nearly impossible and emotionally difficult to perform royal duties like addressing his subjects. In the last scene, he has done a deep dive into what might be driving his speech issues and he makes peace with his inner turmoil, becomes king, largely overcomes his stammer and can calmly address the people of England. He has overcome internal and external obstacles, grown, changed and become a better person. It is a textbook example of the Three-Act Structure used well.

In the first scene of The Social Network, cocky and arrogant Mark Zuckerberg's girlfriend is breaking up with him, saying she thinks they should be friends, to which he replies "I don't need friends." In the last scene, Zuckerberg has created Facebook, become wealthy, set fire to many bridges, remains cocky and arrogant but, in the final shot, sends a friend request to the young woman who dumped him at the start of the film. Has Zuckerberg grown, changed and improved as a person? So, does it follow the Three-Act Structure in the conventional sense? In Django Unchained (2012), the protagonist is much changed and much improved when you compare him at the beginning to him at the end but almost any resemblance to the Three-Act Structure ends there.

It has always interested me that Tom McCarthy's wonderful, relatively low-budget, distinctly "indie" debut The Station Agent (2003) really follows the Three-Act Structure pretty faithfully, but his Oscar-winning big-budget, more mainstream film Spotlight (2015) does not follow it in the conventional sense. Who is the main character in Spotlight? Does he or she grow and change as a person in the end? Birdman (2014)? Is Sgt. James a better person at the end of The Hurt Locker (2008)? People like to fight me on this point, but I lean toward it: screenplays that think outside of the box can win—and frequently do—win Oscars. Okay, let's not get ahead of ourselves. micro-budget films of the kind we are talking about making usually do not get nominated for Oscars.

Noam Kroll came to writing after establishing himself as more technically oriented.

> I came more from a camera angle, but, when I first got into writing, kind of resisted -like every filmmaker- Three-Act Structure, you want to do everything your own way. And, and you realize after a while that you can play within those lines and be completely unique and different, but also adhere to these principles that have existed for thousands of years in storytelling and exist for a reason because they mimic human life. You know, human life has a beginning, a middle and an end, all of us, whether we're trying to navigate getting a new job or getting a divorce or having a kid, we go through these phases of essentially a beginning, middle and end like The Hero's Journey, the Joseph Campbell stuff and the poetics and all this stuff that everybody kind of comes back to. I definitely believe that structure is incredibly important and Three-Act Structure is one method of creating a format that your story can follow. But I like to also

embrace other structures as well when I'm writing. I definitely feel that having any sort of goal posts that you can hit along the way that allow you to, at least, create some boundaries to work with and that can be actually really liberating. I think if you have a great story and you're trying to force a square peg in a round hole and get an inciting incident on page 12, when it should really be on page 14, I feel like that can really hinder your creativity because I think it is really important for filmmakers who are writing and producing and directing their own material to remember, is that a lot of the screenwriting advice that people give is actually geared toward people who want to specifically just be professional screenwriters and their path is very different. They're not trying to make those movies, they're trying to option them or use them as calling cards. Yes, there is a case to be made about, okay, you want to hit this on page 12 or this on page 50, because you might have a reader who is looking for those things, but if you're making your own film and it doesn't feel right to do that, then you're essentially going to be making a decision based on essentially a standard from a different industry almost entirely or a different subsect of your own industry instead of instead of embracing the choices that that would best benefit of what you're trying to do, which is, is actually making the film.

I am not against the Three-Act Structure. I have even come out of films and thought to myself, "That film would have worked better if they had gone with a more conventional Three-Act Structure approach to the story." That said, on a micro-budget production, this formula might not be the best approach.

Lawrence Michael Levine writes, produces and directs his own films, but he makes his living as a screenwriter for hire and he touched on the topic of Three-Act Structure:

> When I'm working on more conventional stuff, I definitely use a Three-Act Structure. And I use an eight sequence structure we have, which is like eight plans. And each plan gets messed

up. And then a new plan has to be formed at the end of every sequence, is kind of my approach to things. But not in the films that I've directed. The only one that utilized it was Wild Canaries (2014), which is kind of a caper movie. And it needs that kind of structure. It definitely needs Three-Act Act Structure. Mysteries are very structural, even if they're a joke and I find mystery writing very, very structural. It has to be very plot oriented.

Now, there is another school of thought that promotes not having any consciousness of the "rules" of screenwriting and just letting screenplays flow organically. I get it on one level, but, from experience, on a practical level, it can make the job much harder than it needs to be. I have read too many rambling, unwieldy, stream-of-consciousness screenplays to be fully supportive of this approach. It is kind of like handing a guitar to someone who does not know how to play it and then expecting music to be created. I can see taking this approach in early sketching sessions, looking for beats and getting a feel for the story, but, in terms of practical screenwriting, actually sitting down and writing something, I think it can pose problems.

Back to the "rules" of the Three-Act Structure, this model has been the industry standard for a long time. Why? On one level, since the publication of Syd Field's Screenplay in 1979, aspiring screenwriters have felt like they have a roadmap or, okay, I will say it, a paradigm for learning how to write a screenplay. It was not only aspiring screenwriters who flocked to the book, but it was, to some degree, the movie business. Remember, in 1979, we were a few years into the "neo-blockbuster" era where, perhaps more than ever, major motion pictures had to be so much more than mere movies, they had to generate merchandise sales. There seems to have been this perception that Field had unlocked the secrets to making a successful film so that all anyone had to do was follow his Three-Act Structure Paradigm in their screenplay and get that much closer to having a better chance of having a hit. Movies cost a lot of money to make and people do not want to lose money, so anything that seemed like a formula for success would be embraced. Look at the films of the

1970s as compared to the 1980s. By 1985 or so, it seems like most mainstream films were following the "Paradigm" closely.

No, Field did not necessarily invent this stuff on his own, there were other teachers discussing the same thing with slightly different language, something which persists to this day, but he was the first or one of the first to put everything down in a book. Most books on screenwriting all say the same thing in a different way. In Field's 2013 New York Times obituary, it said "The term "plot point" appeared in The New York Times fewer than ten times during the century or so before 1979. Since then, it has appeared more than 200 times."

Back to formula and "rules," if you were in Hamburg, Germany, in the early 1960s and went out to see a band in a club, you might have seen a group called The Beatles. At first, The Beatles were a cover band, doing two- to three-minute-long pop songs by American musicians. Even if you are not a musician, if you have any familiarity with popular music, you probably know the structure that 95% of all pop songs take:

Verse
Chorus
Verse
Chorus
Bridge
Lead Break
Verse
Chorus

The Beatles performed six or seven nights a week, sometimes spending as much as eight hours onstage over the course of a night. It is not hard to imagine that, after playing covers of pop songs for hours and hours and hours, the band had a pretty fair understanding of the structure of the form. Their first few albums were a mix of covers and originals, eventually giving way to more and more originals. After more than a few years of writing and recording two- to three-minute pop songs, they knew the form inside and out, backward and forward, up and down and they revolutionized popular music with deep experimentation and sophistication.

So, even if you do not plan to follow the "rules" of screenwriting, I think it is important to know them inside out, up, down, backward and forward. With that philosophy in mind and as briefly as possible, let's take a look at the conventional Three–Act Structure. In this model, screenplays are broken down into, that's right, Three Acts. Usually, the First and Third Acts are each half as long as the Second Act, so you might have a 30-minute first act, a 60-minute second act and a 30-minute Third Act. Rather than Beginning, Middle and End, we say Set-Up, Conflict and Resolution. In the First Act, you introduce all or most of the main characters and put your protagonist in conflict or crisis. In the Second Act, the protagonist takes action to resolve the conflict through trial and error, usually failing miserably by the end of the act. In the Third Act, the protagonist licks their wounds, picks themselves up and gives it one more try, often tapping into some hidden strength, overcoming a major internal flaw, rising to the challenge and succeeding in the end.

Now, those are just the broad strokes and they apply to almost any story, so let's break it down even further. I am not sure what came first, the unwritten rule that anyone in the business will read the first ten pages of any screenplay and, if after ten pages, they are not hooked, they stop reading or the practice of screenwriters to front-load their first ten pages with all kinds of hook-worthy story beats. I suspect it was the former first and then writers started tailoring their first ten pages to get past the gatekeepers.

So, the first ten pages are supposed to set the tone of the film, establish the genre, introduce all or most major characters, give a sense of where the story is going to go and, most importantly, have an Inciting Incident, the big beat that gets the story going, frequently something that shocks the protagonist out of their comfort zone and forces them to take action.

Some common inciting incidents include:

Getting fired
Getting hired

Getting dumped

Getting unexpected news

Meeting an attractive new person

Being bitten by a genetically modified spider

Having your son kidnapped by fishermen and taken to a dentist's office in Sydney

It has been said that good stories come from good characters. If you know your characters well enough, you will have a good sense of how they will respond to a crisis. Quick, who is the antagonist in Rocky? William Faulkner said, "The only thing worth writing about is the human heart in conflict with itself." Rocky Balboa is his own worst enemy and, to me, he is the true antagonist. Now, that's a good character. Next, give the character a crisis that will test them and force them to confront flaws and weaknesses. In most conventional Three-Act Structure screenplays, the character grows and changes, usually for the better. In Tootsie (1982), Dustin Hoffman's character, Michael Dorsey, is a male chauvinist at the beginning and, at the end, he has a more enlightened view of women.

So, give your characters room for growth, flaws they need to fix and wounds that they need to heal. Think of your Three-Act screenplay as a Before and After advertisement. At the beginning of the film, when we first see the protagonist, he or she is often much different at the end of the film. Many protagonists have an emotional void left by the loss of a loved one, which is a device to almost automatically breed sympathy for your main character. Why do you think so many Disney and Marvel characters are missing one or more parents?

So, in the first ten minutes of 95% of all mainstream films, we usually meet a sympathetic, kind of needy protagonist with an emotional void. The character's life is thrown out of whack by an inciting incident. After trying to make sense of the new situation created by the Inciting Incident, around 30 minutes into the film, the protagonist makes a conscious decision to pursue some kind of resolution. Note that it is important to keep in mind that the Inciting Incident is something that happens to the protagonist and the decision he or she makes at First Act Break is something they choose to do. Usually, that decision winds up being faulty, leaving the protagonist in worse shape at the end of the Second Act than he or she was in when we first met them. In the Third Act, the protagonist regroups and attacks the issue with more tenacity, often risking literal or figurative death to succeed, usually becoming a better person in the process.

## Conventional Three-Act Structure Character Arc

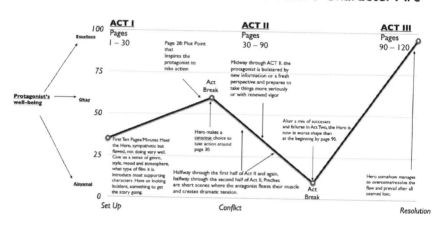

Let's get even more granular by breaking down a film. In School of Rock (2004), Dewey Finn (Jack Black) is an obnoxious, somewhat delusional rock star wannabe. The audience knows these things about him even before he has his first real line of dialogue. He acts like he is headlining Madison Square Garden when the reality is that, when we first see him, his band is playing to a sparse, indifferent collection of bar patrons. Even the other musicians in his band appear to dislike him.

In the second scene, we discover that Dewey is broke, crashing at a friend/former bandmate's apartment and has not paid rent for a long time. His roommate, Ned (played by the film's screenwriter Mike White) gives him an ultimatum: get a job or get out. Dewey says that the band is about to hit it big, win an upcoming Battle of the Bands competition and get rich, thus stating Dewey's conscious external goal: win the Battle of the Bands and become a rock star and establishing his unconscious internal goal: get real and grow up. When Dewey chides him for being a substitute teacher, Ned responds with

"You think it's so easy, I'd like to see you try; you wouldn't last a day." Spoiler Alert: Dewey winds up masquerading as Ned and taking a job as a teacher. Ned's line gives the audience a sense of what is going to happen in the film.

Next, in the third scene, an inciting incident: Dewey is fired from the band, dashing his hopes of winning the competition, paying back Ned and taking a step closer toward becoming a rock star. Now, Dewey has to find a new band. In the meantime, he answers a call for Ned from a school that needs a substitute. Dewey pretends that he is Ned and accepts the job in order to make some quick cash.

At the end of ten minutes, there is an inciting incident. We have met Dewey, Ned, Ned's girlfriend, Dewey's old bandmates, the principal of the school and all of his students.

The next major plot point usually comes in at around page 28, when a character is motivated to take action based on the situation presented by the Inciting Incident. Around 28 minutes into the film, Dewey sends his students off to music class. With time on his hands, he peeks into their classroom and sees that most of them can play an instrument. Around page 30, he has decided that he is going to use the students as his new band. This bad decision comes to a head at the end of the Second Act, when he is exposed and even threatened with legal action. In the end, his students rally around him, they perform at Battle of the Bands but lose to Dewey's old band. Cut to sometime in the near future, Dewey has opened The School of Rock, where he gives lessons to kids. He has failed at his attempt to become a rock star—his external, conscious goal—but he has somehow managed to mature into a successful business owner who can pay his bills while still indulging his love of rock music—his internal, unconscious goal or need. Final shot of the film: he is surrounded by musicians who love him, contrasting the first scene of the film.

We all know that Aristotle defined a story as something with a unified beginning, middle and end. Later, Jean–Luc Goddard amended that statement with his own "Every story has a beginning, middle and end but not necessarily in that order." Just keep in mind that, while it seems like many, many films follow the Three-Act Structure, there is no law stating that you have to use it. That said, even if you do not use the Three-Act Structure, your story does need some rhyme and reason, some kind of structure and an organized order of events.

In a micro-budget film, where there are usually no big set pieces or special effects to dazzle the audience, story structure and construction become even more important. On a micro-budget film, your story and the way it unfolds are usually your primary "special effect." You have to make sure that the drama is compelling and surprising, so, without overdoing it, twists in the narrative can become fuel to keep your plot moving. If you are making a micro-budget comedy, you have to be really funny most of the time. If you are making a horror film, you have to be scary or, at least, ominous, most of the time. In a micro-budget film, there is no time for filler or wasted scenes that do not go anywhere. I am not saying that your comedy has to be wall-to-wall laughs or that your horror film has to be wall-to-wall scares but that you have to make sure that the moments between the laughs and the scares cannot be throwaways.

Look at the conventional structure of a horror movie: something scary happens in the first scene and then, for the most part, nothing really scary happens until 30, 40 and 45 minutes into the story. In a micro-budget film with limited locations and characters, you are often already at risk of testing the audience's patience, so you are advised not to have 30–45 minutes where nothing really happens. The relatively micro-budgeted ($130,000) 2003 film Open Water built its marketing campaign on the fact that the production used real sharks to terrorize a couple of divers left at sea when their charter boat departed without them. The film is about 80 minutes long and, as I recall, there are no sharks in it for the first 35 minutes or so and, even then, they only show up occasionally. So, what does that leave us with? A not particularly compelling domestic drama for the first 35 minutes that continues, albeit with interruptions from the sharks, for the rest of the film. To reiterate, this is an 80-minute film, ostensibly about a couple terrorized by sharks, but there are no sharks for the first half of the film. In other words, it feels like this film is half filler.

Okay, there are a number of finer points that I left out of this example, but, if you really wanted to learn conventional, industry-standard story structure, you probably would not still be reading this book.

How all of this applies to writing micro-budget screenplays is really important here.

By nature, in a conventional Three-Act screenplay, not much can happen in the plot between the inciting incident and the plot point on page 28, it is sort of wasted space leading up to the Second Act, when the story kicks into high gear. In a micro-budget film, you often cannot afford to have as much as 20 or 25 minutes where nothing really happens. Because micro-budget films tend to run 90 minutes or less, those pages after the inciting incident become more valuable in terms of plot.

## Conventional Three-Act Structure Act I

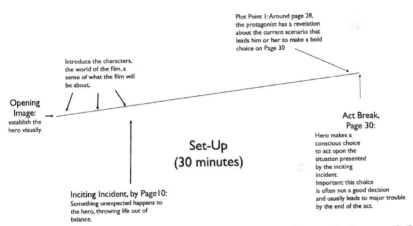

Plot Point 1: Around page 28, the protagonist has a revelation about the current scenario that leads him or her to make a bold choice on Page 30

Introduce the characters, the world of the film, a sense of what the film will be about.

Opening Image: establish the hero visually.

**Set-Up (30 minutes)**

Act Break, Page 30:
Hero makes a conscious choice to act upon the situation presented by the inciting incident. Important: this choice is often not a good decision and usually leads to major trouble by the end of the act.

Inciting Incident, by Page 10:
Something unexpected happens to the hero, throwing life out of balance.

# What happens between Page 10 and Page 28?

Here is where you could start thinking about alternatives to structure that will better serve your film. Also, because of the low budget, there is only so much you can do in terms of keeping things moving with location changes and adding minor characters. You need to keep your film going by making more things happen in your screenplay, especially in this first third of the story. So, rather than waiting for the major plot point on page 28 and the Act Break on page 30, strongly consider employing multiple big—but not huge plot points throughout the act. Throw in complications, revelations and issues for your characters to deal with early on so that you can avoid those frequently deadly long scenes of people bantering back and forth. Stuff has to happen. Because you cannot afford big set pieces or special effects, you need more drama in the first act to keep the film engaging.

## Theoretical Structure for Act I of a Micro-Budget Film

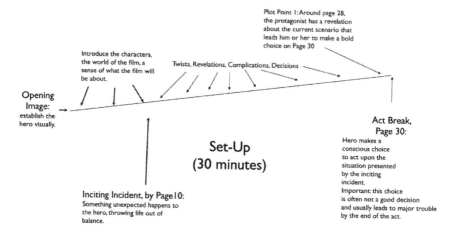

Plot Point 1: Around page 28, the protagonist has a revelation about the current scenario that leads him or her to make a bold choice on Page 30

Introduce the characters, the world of the film, a sense of what the film will be about.

Twists, Revelations, Complications, Decisions

Opening Image: establish the hero visually.

Act Break, Page 30:

Set-Up (30 minutes)

Hero makes a conscious choice to act upon the situation presented by the inciting incident. Important: this choice is often not a good decision and usually leads to major trouble by the end of the act.

Inciting Incident, by Page 10: Something unexpected happens to the hero, throwing life out of balance.

Personally, I think that, if you are spending money to produce a film, you should avoid wasting it through not being prepared with any sense of what to do, where to do it and who to have do it.

The topic of story structure came up with Jim Byrkit, too.

DG: You built it on the foundation of structure and yet there was this freedom to go off on tangents.

JB: The only reason I knew that I could allow for the tangents was because I had the structure underneath, I knew that it would survive, and still get to the end and tell the story, even if this couple started arguing, or even if this guy started being a lot more sarcastic than I thought, or even if this person was a lot more emotional. If you know, the structure is there, then you know that there, you're still on the path. So the specifics of the arguments and whatnot, might not have mattered as long as they were still going in the right direction. I started out being utterly anti structural, I couldn't stand the idea of there being you know, rules or templates or guidelines. We spent a year really figuring it out scene by scene, it became very classically structured. I realized that in order to do the things that I was interested in doing, which were pushing the boundaries of what had been done, the only way to keep those understandable for an audience was to pin them on some kind of structure. So I learned very slowly that structure could be my friend and I could still do all the creative things I wanted to do, using that as a backbone.

Introducing the character, having you know, in Coherence, she's given the call to adventure. Very quickly, the guy says, "Hey, come to Vietnam with me." She refuses the call to adventure, all those little things? We didn't make them quite so obvious as a normal film. It's not Luke Skywalker, getting the offer from the mentor. So everything is there. But it's just not quite as obvious as a typical Hollywood film. But by having it there, by having the structure there, you can then judge when you're editing. Why isn't this working? Why? Why did we seem to have a scene that doesn't fit and if you keep comparing it to the structure, keep comparing it to a template, you can then decide what to keep and what not to keep. So Coherence actually really, really follows classic structure almost perfectly, it's just not as apparent, not because of style. She has an ordeal absolutely, a transformative experience that could only happen through this story. And the only things that the storyteller reveals to the audience are the things that you need to understand how she got there. It's just like a campfire story. If you're telling it as a campfire story, you tell it just like so. So this girl shows up at a party, and you start giving only the information to understand how you got from A to B.

While there is not enough space to take a deep dive into scene dynamics in this book, because your film is going to be made up of scenes, we should take a little look.

It's tempting to say that a 120-page script at approximately two to three pages per scene should have 40–60 scenes. While not wrong, this is a gross generalization.

The better answer is that a screenplay should have as many scenes as are necessary to tell the story, but no more.

For the sake of laying a foundation, let's define a scene as generally thought of as the action in a single location and continuous time. Anytime the crew needs to break down the lights, camera, sound, etc., pack them all up, move to a new location and set everything up again; it is usually because it is time to shoot a new scene. It is important to keep this concept in mind when making a micro-budget film because, when time and money are at a premium, you might want to consider the number of times you have to perform this routine. No, I am not saying that your film should have five 20-minute scenes, but that you should be conscious of how much time you will need to allow for company moves.

Scenes are made up of beats. A beat is an exchange of behavior in action/reaction.

A scene is like a miniature model of the story itself; in that it also has an act structure: Beginning, Middle and End or Set-up, Conflict and Resolution. Most scenes include the protagonist or the antagonist. Every Scene is About the Hero (even if he or she is not in the scene). Each Scene Chronicles the Hero's Quest. Scenes should create anticipation.

Byrkit talked about the importance of having only scenes that serve the story in Coherence.

> One of the traps that filmmakers fall into, especially on their first films is that they have scenes that are interesting to them, but they don't actually forward the story or thicken the tension in any way. And so we knew that because we had such a limited range of resources that every scene had to escalate it, somehow every scene had to be a piece of the puzzle. So, if you work backwards from the end of the film, and say, "What is her end state?" Every single scene in the film then shows you how she got step by step from the first shot to the last shot. And if something didn't really further that path, then it was extraneous, and probably got cut.

A great example of the way scenes work can be found in Tony Gilroy's masterful screenplay for The Bourne Identity (2002). In every scene, Jason Bourne is either looking for information, acting on information he has found or defending himself against the bad guys. The scenes of Bourne alternate with the scenes of the bad guys tracking him, looking for information about him or acting upon information they find.

They do not take credit for this concept, but there is a great, two-minute video from MTV U. on YouTube that shows South Park creators Trey Parker and Matt Stone talking about scenes to a class at NYU. They make the point that, if the words "and then" can be written between your scenes, you are in danger of having a boring screenplay. Instead, they say, either the word "but" or "therefore" should come between your scenes. When you outline, you should not be writing "this happens AND THEN that happens AND THEN this happens AND THEN that happens," you should be writing "this happens BUT that happens THEREFORE this happens BUT that happens THEREFORE this happens" and so on. Take this approach and the chances of writing a dynamic screenplay improve dramatically.

Scenes typically have four possible functions:

- Forward either a story's plot, one of its subplots, or both
- Reveal or explore a character's personality or behavior through their actions
- Introduce or deepen thematic ideas
- Give expository information

If a scene is not doing one or more of the previously mentioned things, it should be cut.

Director Mike Nichols once said, "Every scene should be a fight, a seduction, or a negotiation."

The question of how long a scene should be is a tough one and, while there is no hard and fast right or wrong answer, in a micro-budget film, it has to be a major consideration in some ways that differ from bigger-budgeted productions. Remember when we used to buy DVDs and sometimes the disc was promoted by advertising that it includes anywhere from five to ten or more deleted scenes? That means that someone signed off on a budget to produce a screenplay that had five to ten scenes that could ultimately be cut from the final film and not dramatically affect the story. Keep in mind that the average major film costs $80,000,000 to make, productions aim to shoot three to four pages of screenplay a day. Honestly, you could probably make a micro-budget film for the amount of money that was spent on producing one of those scenes that were cut from the film. The point here is that, in a micro-budget screenplay, there is little room for throwaway scenes that could or could not fit into the final cut, so write them carefully. You cannot afford to write, cast, shoot and edit scenes that you do not really need. Look at every scene and ask yourself "Would the movie still make sense without this scene?" If the answer is "yes," then you don't really need the scene, shouldn't bother writing it and, if you have written it, think about cutting it.

So, how long should a scene be? Short, in general. How short is short? Conventional wisdom says that a scene should be about a maximum of two to three pages/minute. As recently as the late 1990s, the average scene was three pages/minute. Today, the average scene is 1.5 pages/minute. Keep in mind that some scenes are only 1/8 of a page, while others might be four to five pages. If, when I am writing a scene, it gets to the bottom of page 3 and I am not finished, I know that I am in "trouble" and, if appropriate, I break the scene up into sub-scenes as illustrated in Chapter 4.

The big takeaway here is that, in a Micro-budget film where you are usually less likely to be able to captivate and dazzle the audience with special effects, stunts and set pieces, your story is the main thing you have going for you. Pump up that story. Now, to be clear, you do not need to bang the audience over their heads with a barrage of content; you do not need to go overboard and veer too close to melodrama; you just have to be especially conscientious of things happening in your film because, in the end, your story is the main thing that is keeping your film going.

Now, all of that said, Vera Brunner–Sung's Bella Vista (2014) adheres to almost none of it and I loved the film. There is no inciting incident, we know almost nothing about the main character, she seems to have a sliver of backstory, but there is no clear, tangible external goal, no definitive emotional void and no unconscious internal goal; there is not much in the way of drama or conflict and the end? I am not even going to discuss the end. The film really challenged conventions of what a film is supposed to be and really opened my eyes to what a film can be, maybe what more films should be. I was not sure what to expect when I interviewed her, but, as soon as she told me about her background, everything about the film fell into place and made sense in my mind.

Vera Brunner–Sung: My background is an experimental documentary. I went to CalArts, and I studied with James Benning and Tom Anderson. And I really thought I was the kind of a one–woman band filmmaker. So that was the sensibility that I brought to the writing. And while the sensibility was, "who cares how you're supposed to write a script?"

# 6
# MODEL YOUR FEATURE ON A SHORT

Remember, originally, all films were short films. A film was about as long as the amount of celluloid on a reel, around ten minutes. In the early 1900s, people began to realize that they could start combining these ten-minute reels into longer films. Up through the 1970s, it was not uncommon for a studio-produced short film to accompany a feature in a theater.

Making short films can be like a training camp for a feature. Shorts are a great way to experiment with shots, effects and editing. Making a short can also be an effective way to see how well you work or do not work well with members of your crew.

But you should consider shorts on a much deeper level. First, and importantly, short films are an art form in their own right. Looking at shorts can be priceless when looking at ways to approach your micro-budget Feature.

Allow me a little diversion. Think about your favorite poem. You have a favorite poem, don't you? Okay, if not, for the sake of example, take a look at Robert Frost's Stopping By Woods on a Snowy Evening

This poem is one of the most famous poems by one of America's most famous poets. Would it have worked better as a novel? Of course not. Poetry and Fiction are two different art forms that have many qualities in common. Both forms utilize words to create and imply mood and imagery.

DOI: 10.4324/9781003138969-7

Similarly, short films and features both usually employ some degree of cinematography, sound and/or editing—not to mention the occasional actor and dialogue. My point here is that short films and features should be considered separate art forms and not compared to each other. Yes, a short film can resemble a truncated feature, but, in my experience, shorts are most effective when they are not trying to emulate the narrative scope of a feature in a fraction of the time.

Years ago, when I was reviewing films for a trade publication, I came across a bad horror film that seemed like it had been adapted from a five-minute short. In other words, the story of the feature only worked for about five minutes. By pure coincidence, not long after, I somehow found myself up for a screenwriting gig by the director of the bad horror film. I do not know exactly what got into me, but I mentioned that I had seen the horror film and that it seemed like they had a five-minute film and tried to squeeze a feature out of it. He responded by saying "We had a five minute film and tried to squeeze a feature out of it." We chuckled about it. He was amused. His producer was not amused, and I did not get the gig. I guess that "If you see something, say something" does not apply in cases like this one.

Next, sometimes it seems like many people think of shorts as mini-features or, maybe more commonly, the teaser trailer, not a work of art on their own but more like a commercial for a work of art.

I am split on teaser trailers. A producer I know was having lunch in L.A. with the producing partner of a major A-list actor/director/producer. She wanted to pitch him a project and asked if he would read a one-page synopsis. No. Would he read a half-page synopsis? No. Would he read a logline? No. Would he watch a ninety-second teaser trailer? Sure. Nice story but I think it is a pretty extraordinary situation. If you have a cast, location and a crew to make a teaser trailer, I think you should hold off until you can make a feature with all of them. Can't afford to make the feature version? Chances are slim that the project is something that you can get financing for. My suggestion is, make a micro-budget film instead.

I have just seen too many people put too much energy into making a teaser trailer and hoping for financing when they could have spent that time on making a micro-budget feature. Yes, there are famous cases of teaser trailers being the key to getting financing. Whiplash (2014) comes to mind, but the teaser trailer story is only part of what happened. Damien Chazelle was not a complete unknown by the time he was trying to make Whiplash and the feature version of the screenplay was already attracting some attention. So, yes, the teaser trailer—actually just a short scene from the feature—did help with financing, but what helped more was that, while not exactly an insider, he was not exactly an outsider. Personally, I would be cautious about putting too much time and energy into a teaser trailer.

Next, if you are in film school or a film school graduate, chances are good that you have some experience with making a senior thesis. The topic of student films came up when I spoke with Alex Ross Perry.

> I spent, probably about $20,000 to $25,000, on my 22 minute, senior thesis. I wrote something as completely ordinary and simple as a scene set in a cafe. But I never forgot this, the cafe that we found, I think charged me $1200 for an overnight, so we got in when they closed, and we're able to shoot until they opened. So we were there, probably 6pm to 8am, or something. And my teacher said, "That's an amazing rate for a location, and it's a one and a half page scene." Wow. And it seemed reasonable, you know, for $1200, you get your location for 12 hours. And then, two years later, when ultra low budget, micro-budget movies are being made into features for $10,000 total, there's no $1200 for one location, one and half pages. That's ludicrous. And I was just like, "the only way you can pull off a 70 minute feature on the budget is you do not write a $1200 check for a single location, unless you're shooting that location for the entire shoot." And that whole $1200 check covers your sole, shooting location, and then the whole crew lived there. If you're paying 5% of your budget, or 10% of your budget for a location, you better be in it for 30% of the movie.

There are standards and approaches that frequently apply to features but do not always work in shorts. That said, after teaching courses on writing short films for nearly 20 years, I have been finding ways to borrow techniques from short films and utilizing them to write features.

In discussing short films, we need to talk about story structure because it can have a significant impact on the way you approach a feature. Looking back over my favorite short films, one of the things that emerge is that few short narrative films follow the Three-Act Structure in the same way that 95% of mainstream features do. Yes, there is a discussion of the Three-Act Structure elsewhere in this book, but, for the sake of illustrating the way it compares to shorts, it makes sense to do a mini-review in this chapter.

As discussed in Chapter 5, in the conventional Three-Act Structure film, the first ten minutes is critical. It is well known that, supposedly, anyone in the business will read the first ten pages of any screenplay and, if it does not tick certain boxes, the reader stops reading. We usually meet a needy, sympathetic protagonist in the first ten minutes of a film and, also within those first ten minutes, something—the inciting incident—throws them out of their comfort zone. About 20 pages/minute later, the protagonist makes a conscious decision about the situation presented by the inciting incident and takes action. Next, there is a series of plot ups and downs, obstacles to overcome, adversaries to face and, usually by the ⅔ or ¾ mark, the protagonist crashes and burns, hits bottom, has to pick up the pieces, tap into some hidden strength, resolve some internal issue, rise to the occasion and resolve the issue of the film.

This approach to story is frequently ineffective when approaching a short film. First, of course, in a ten-minute film, you do not have ten minutes to introduce and establish the protagonist, the setting, an inciting incident and a resolution. Have you ever encountered a short film online, maybe even as short as two minutes long but turned it off? How can you not sit through a short film? Too many people take too long to establish the story in their short films. Well, if it does not grab you from the beginning, chances are you are not going to watch it to the end. So, the key in short films is hooking the audience within the first 15–20 seconds.

One of the best ways to hook an audience quickly is to begin mid-crisis that is after the inciting incident. I have been showing Nash Edgerton's wonderful short film Spider (2007) to classes for years. After screening it, I ask my class what it is about and most students usually answer "It's about a couple having a fight" to which I respond, "Actually, it is about a couple who has had a fight." The fight is the inciting incident that causes the situation in the film, but we never see the fight, we see the aftermath of it. Jim Cummings' much-lauded (and deservedly so) Sundance-winning Best Short Thunder Road (2016) begins at the funeral of the protagonist's mother—her death is the inciting incident. In a shining example of a short that was successfully adapted into a feature, the full-length adaptation of Thunder Road (2018) won Best Feature at South By Southwest but also begins the same way, after the inciting incident.

Yes, you do not have to show the inciting incident in your feature, you can introduce your characters already in conflict, already dealing with a challenging situation. This approach can be extraordinarily effective because the audience comes in late, has to play catch-up and put extra effort into focusing on what is happening and engaging with the story. In a short film, there is no room for superfluous action. Short films have to be lean and mean, brutally efficient in their storytelling.

So, you are starting after the inciting incident. As mentioned, in a feature, the inciting incident usually occurs in the first ten minutes of the film and then there is a period of nearly 20 minutes before the next major plot point on or around page 30. So, what happens in that 20 minutes? A lot of acclimating to the situation. It usually works in a conventional feature, but it will not work in a short film and, in a micro-budget feature, it can be a deadly waste of time. The big lesson here is that, in a short film, the inciting incident can also be like the act break that comes on page 30. The point is that, in a micro-budget film where you will likely have limited visual stimulation from location changes and special effects, you need to keep the story moving and engaging. Consider having your inciting incident as close to the beginning of the film if not before the beginning of the film so that you can engineer something resembling an act break within the first 10–15 minutes instead of coming around page 30.

Next, the ending. When we sit down to watch a feature, we have come to expect a tidy resolution where all of the loose ends of the plot wrap up. Short films frequently leave stories with unresolved characters hanging in limbo. There are no FDA regulations stating that you need to wrap everything up at the end of your micro-budget film. An unresolved ending can be provocative, leaving the audience to wonder "what's next?" and try to fill in the blanks. Audiences have come to expect to be spoon-fed a tidy resolution, and I think it can be fine to deprive them of that closure. Stomping Ground ends with all of the characters facing an uncertain future. Let the audience think about what happens after the final scene.

# Act I

# feature length film

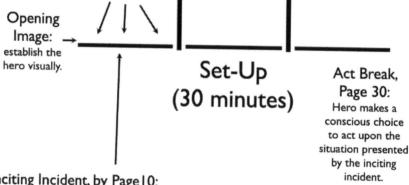

Introduce the characters, the world of the film, a sense of what the film will be about.

Opening Image: → establish the hero visually.

**Set-Up (30 minutes)**

Act Break, Page 30: Hero makes a conscious choice to act upon the situation presented by the inciting incident.

Inciting Incident, by Page 10: Something unexpected happens to the hero, throwing life out of balance.

# Act I
## short film

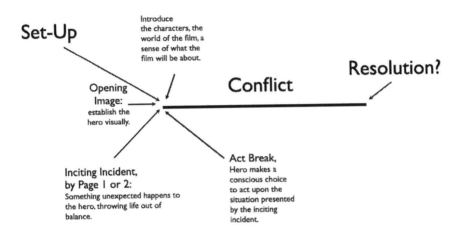

Set-Up

Introduce the characters, the world of the film, a sense of what the film will be about.

Opening Image: establish the hero visually.

**Conflict**

Resolution?

Inciting Incident, by Page 1 or 2: Something unexpected happens to the hero, throwing life out of balance.

Act Break, Hero makes a conscious choice to act upon the situation presented by the inciting incident.

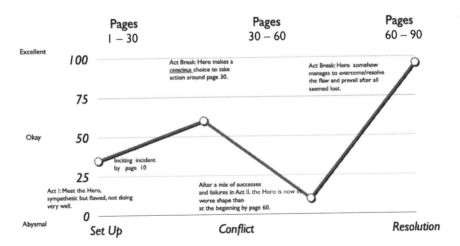

Pages 1 – 30

Pages 30 – 60

Pages 60 – 90

Excellent — 100

Act Break: Hero makes a conscious choice to take action around page 30.

Act Break: Hero somehow manages to overcome/resolve the flaw and prevail after all seemed lost.

75

Okay — 50

Inciting incident by page 10

25

Act I: Meet the Hero, sympathetic but flawed, not doing very well.

After a mix of successes and failures in Act II, the Hero is now in worse shape than at the beginning by page 60.

Abysmal — 0

Set Up

Conflict

Resolution

# Character Arc
## feature length film

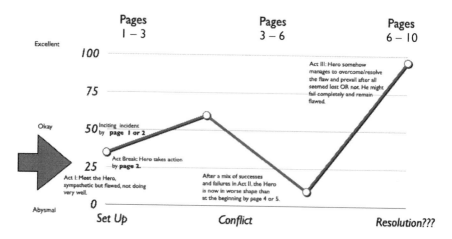

# Character Arc
## short film

## Theoretical Structure for Act I of a Micro-Budget Film

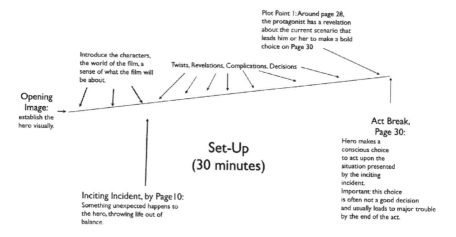

I am starting to see more and more features that borrow from shorts in this manner. As mentioned in another chapter, much in the way that some people like indie, underground music, I spend a lot of time browsing for indie, out of the mainstream or underground films.

One of the most exciting trends going on now is the increase in the number of what some people call Medium-Length Films. These frequently low-budget, homespun films are usually in the 60–80 minute range and, in the streaming era, where sometimes you do not want to commit to a two-hour film at 11 PM, a 75-minute-long film can look appealing. Many of these films employ some of the techniques characteristic of short films that I described earlier—opting against the conventional Three-Act Structure, an accelerated beginning, a break into the second act long before the 30-minute mark and vague, unresolved endings.

The topic came up when I spoke with Aaron Katz, who might have unwittingly been part of the first wave in the modern era of Medium-Length Films with Dance Party USA (2006).

> I have to say, honestly, the movie wasn't intended to be 66 minutes long, I'm pretty sure the script was like 105 pages or 110. . . . I thought it was a 90 minute feature. And once it got down to 66 minutes, which it felt like it had to because that's what made sense. But I remember feeling like just crying, honestly, kind of devastated that Dance Party was only 66 minutes long. I was like, "it's not a short, it's not a feature." That length of movie was generally not seen as very legit, except for a lot of Roger Corman and grindhouse stuff but High Noon is 80 minutes. I remember looking at the Sundance guidelines, and being like, "the Sundance guidelines say a feature needs to be at least 70 minutes long. And instead of just writing "TRT, 70 minutes" on the DVD, or whatever, I was like, "Oh, it's only 66 minutes." I guess I had submitted it as a short, and of course, got rejected. But I remember feeling like that it felt like a rejection of that it was even a real movie. I'm sure we had an 85 or 90 minute cut that felt really flat and really not good. And I think, on instinct, we're just kind of just chiseling away at it till whatever was left was good. And we were sitting at this 60-something minute runtime, and I was just like, "Is there anything to put back in here?" Not even because I thought it was a good idea, but because it felt really

depressing that it wasn't a normal length. In retrospect, I like that length. Quiet City (2007), which is 78 minutes, is still in that ballpark, it feels good. But I just kept submitting it to festivals. I got rejected from Sundance, as a short rejected from Slamdance. And then we got into South by Southwest. Matt Dentler, who was the programmer there is like, the reason that any of us—Swanberg, Barry Jenkins, Lena Dunham—got to play our movies. I think Dentler was like, "I want to program this kind of movie, like, I want to find new and young and unheard of people."

Fun Fact: Aaron Katz shot part of his 2019 film Gemini in his house, which is the same house Jim Byrkit lived in and used for Coherence.

To that point, recently, one of my grad students turned in the outline for her screenplay. I really liked it but knew that there was not enough material for a 90-minute feature. We tried to brainstorm ways to expand subplots and give supporting characters more to do, but, in the end, to me, it felt like we were adding filler, not enhancing the story, so I said "You know what, let's just leave it as-is and say we have a solid 75 minute film."

I spoke with Martha Stephens about the experience of making shorts and how it influenced her feature work.

DG: And do you feel that your experience with short films was help-ful when approaching a feature?

MARTHA STEPHENS: I only made short films in college. So just being on set learning how stuff operates on a set was super helpful. I needed that sort of training to be able to go into feature filmmaking. I never had any proper training on how to write a feature film. So the reason I approached my first movie that way was because I wrote it as like, four short films. And then I wove them together, knowing that I didn't quite have the skill set to plot out a feature film, if that makes sense. So it was a love story, each story has its work but it's more of like a 30 minute story per each story, as opposed to like one big slide.

DG: This is something nobody's said to me before in the interviews for this project, this kind of four short films combined into one feature approach. And I'm sure there's a lot of reasons she did it that way; it keeps things active and engaging. One of the problems I find with Micro Budget films is because they're so limited in scope most of the time there's not much that you can do to expand the world of the film. Many of them do start to feel a bit familiar, like you're spending a lot of time in one location with the same characters.

Remember that Tom DiCillo's indie classic about the making of an indie film Living In Oblivion (1995) was originally a 30-minute short and then they decided to make it into a feature by making two more 30-minute shorts. Fun fact, the producer of the film, Marcus Viscidi, was the producer of the first film I ever worked on, Signs of Life.

It also came up with Polly Shattel: I made a kind of a no-budget film. It was like Short Cuts (1993) by Altman. It was several short stories kind of cut together into one intertwining narrative.

Noam Kroll said,

> One of the films that was sort of an indirect influence for this feature (Psychosynthesis) was an even shorter film that is 52 minutes long called See The Sea (1997) by François Ozon. And I loved that film. It was so simple. It's basically a two–hander, two characters. So minimalist, very creepy. And, if it was a minute longer, it would have been too long. And when films can pack that much into, you know, 45, 50 minutes or 75, 80 minutes can be, that's always sort of a treat.
>
> I think a lot of filmmakers hit this crossroad, especially on this budget level where maybe they can raise 20 grand or 40 grand and they're trying to decide between, "Do I make a really substantial, short film that's 25 minutes or 30 minutes and it's got really great production value and it'll be this great calling card or do I just extend it a little more? I have the crew, I could shoot for twice as many days and I could turn this into a 75 minute, 80

minute film, and then it's a feature." I'm not going to tell anyone what to do, but I obviously tend to lean toward feeling like if you're going to make a, a short film that's 25 or 30 minutes, why not make one that's two minutes or that's three minutes because those films are more likely to get programmed at a major film festival than a 30 minute short film.

He continued:

I watch a lot of French New Wave films and even old silent films. And you go back to the origins of cinema. A lot of films were these shorter feature films, or they were 40 minutes. They were 70 minutes. And there's no reason why we have to be boxed into feeling like if it's not 90 minutes on the dot, it's not a feature film because I can list plenty of films that are 90 or longer that, you know, wouldn't hold a candle to other films that you are, I might love that are seventy-five minutes, eighty minutes that are iconic feature films, like broke new ground. So, you know, I think that understanding that is super important, embracing it.

Just as a practical tip for writing, but I think a lot of new writers sort of take the rule of one page per minute, very literally. And they don't realize that a page of dialogue versus a page of action are very different. And some people write a 77 page script. You might be working on something that perhaps has a really healthy mix of action scenes and dialogue scenes where someone might write something that's all dialogue that is 77 pages. But even if they keep in every frame, it might be a 52 minute movie because the characters talk fast. So I think like understanding the mechanics of it, it's so important to just actually get the runtime that you're looking for. But yeah, I agree with you, nobody should ever, in my opinion, be afraid of these shorter feature films. I think less is more. Personally, I'd rather see a great 77 minute film than a mediocre 90. I think one of the reasons I probably gravitate to these Micro Budget films is because you have the ability to do that, to not wrap things up. Oftentimes, when people watch my films, whether they're short films I've made, or in this case, Psychosynthesis, the thing that people often say is like, I feel like it was just start-ing. Like, I feel like you ended it when the movie was starting and when I wanted to see where it was going to go and it's never my intention to frustrate people in that way, but I guess my intention is always to leave things open–ended. I think that the best films that I enjoy the most are the films that wrap up enough that you feel there was a conclusion to the story that you're following.

But with that conclusion, open up a whole other can of worms and questions about where this would now go. I think, uh, if you can, if you can balance that, those are some of the best films. Getting back to the Micro Budget format, you can try to leave some, some things a little bit looser at the end, you can kind of leave some question marks open, um, when, when you're not having to, um, think like a big studio movie.

All ten of Bob Byington's films come in at 80 minutes or less. "You know, the movies are pretty short, the movies end up being like 77 minutes, because I think I'm just terrified of having a feeling they go on too long or for the movie to drag on."

A friend of mine just finished a feature, and there were a lot of issues because the running time was something like 80 minutes, 81 minutes, and the executive producer had a fit saying, "You know, you're contractually obligated to turn in a 90 minute film." And they went to court on that, even though, if you ask me, it doesn't need another second, but now they have to find ways to puff it up to 90 minutes and it just seems ridiculous.

So, do I think there is a future for Medium–Length Films? I hope so. There was a time midway through the pandemic in 2020, when all the movie theaters closed, there was talk of Amazon and Netflix and Disney buying all the movie theaters, and people would go and have an Amazon or Netflix or Disney experience. And there are so many 70-minute movies on Amazon now, because anybody can put anything on Amazon. And I thought, well, who would go see it?

Nobody would go pay to see a 70-minute movie, but they might go pay to see two 70-minute movies like a double feature. I probably would.

Still, whether you are going to see Medium-Length Films in a theater or streaming them at home, I think that there is much to observe, analyze and learn from these films with regard to story structure, pacing, beginnings and endings that owe something to the way some of the best makers of short films approach the form.

# 7
# GENRE CONSIDERATIONS

Okay, I think we have established the point that, most of the time, you are not going to be able to afford elaborate costumes, stunts, locations, effects and so on. If you have unlimited access to a fancy location, by all means, write a story set in a fancy location. In a micro-budget film, the story has to do the heavy lifting so that is where you really need to focus your energy on coming up with great characters, a great story and great dialogue.

So, something to consider, things to ask yourself before proceeding:

1   What kind of movie is this? What genre does it fall into? Mixed-genre films can be a tough sell because the distributor doesn't know how to market them—which is not to say that you should not make one if you have an idea for one.
2   What other movies are like yours? This is really important. It has been said that nobody wants anything original; they want movies that are like other movies that were big hits. There is the old joke/anecdote about a screenwriter taking a meeting, trying to get an assignment where the producer refers to a current big hit and says "Give me the same thing . . . only different." If you are going to be pitching a movie, you want to be able to say "This is Bad Boys For Life meets 1917," referring to two big hits because, the bottom line is the bottom line—how much the film will cost

DOI: 10.4324/9781003138969-8

compared to how much it is likely to make, based on other similar films.

But you are not going to be pitching your film, you are going to be writing, then making it and you want to be conscious of genre conventions whether or not you are adhering to them or subverting them.

Noam Kroll told me:

> The Micro Budget films that fail are typically the ones that are trying to be a big movie. They're trying to be a scaled down version of, you know, an action thriller or this or that. I don't mean to scapegoat any specific genre because any of them can work on a Micro Budget canvas. You could be more experimental with blending genres if you're making a commentary on something, that there's an angle to it. I think about exploring that because the number one thing that ultimately will help your Micro Budget film is the concept and is differentiating what you're doing from the $10 million movie to $50 million movie, because the Micro Budget films that fail are typically the ones that are trying to be a big movie. They're trying to be a scaled down version of an action thriller or this or that. I don't mean to scapegoat any specific genre because any of them can work on a Micro Budget canvas, but I do think that you're better off when you embrace the limitations as opposed to try to pretend that they're not there and try to make your production or your, even the writing of your film resemble a much larger budget feature, because then you're not really taking advantage of the smaller canvas that you're working on. I would probably use my more recent film uh Psychosynthesis as a, as an example, because that's a film that really blends these two genres. So on the one hand, um, when you watch the trailer, it probably comes across more like a traditional genre film, like it's a horror or a thriller, and there are elements of that, but what I think makes the film interesting, and the reason I wanted to make this go home and write this film is because it also infuses this dramatic component.

Not long ago, I watched a low-budget heist thriller on a major streaming platform. Never mind that is was badly written and acted, highly derivative of big-budget films in the same genre—in fact shooting in some of the same locations as a much-revered film in the same genre and even referring to a character from that film, the biggest insult was the attempt at bigger budget stunts and effects that the filmmakers could not afford.

In one scene, a character is "thrown" to his death from the top of a parking garage. The actor is led to the edge of the garage and, in the next shot, he is lying on the ground, dead. Audiences are sophisticated today, if someone is thrown off the top of a building, they expect to see a stunt man execute the stunt. Similarly, while, to some audiences in 2004, adding muzzle shots and blood in post-production with Adobe After Effects might have been passable, nobody buys it anymore. If your production cannot afford a stunt, do not fake it. If your production cannot afford blanks for gunfire and squibs for blood, do not show characters getting shot. I wrote a screenplay where a climactic gunfight happens in the woods at night. From a distance, you can shoot "gunfire" or something flashy in the dark and add sound effects later.

Certain genres present more challenges than others, so, if you want to work in one of them, your screenplay is going to have to be especially inventive. Earlier in the book, I discussed the differences between low-budget film noir and low-budget monster movies. Film noir found ways to use their shortcomings to their advantage, while many monster movies are laughably bad because they could only afford low-rent costumes and effects.

Science fiction films usually conjure up images of intergalactic space battles, gleaming high-tech-looking sets, futuristic costumes and so on. Sure, with a lot of time spent on finding creative work-arounds, you can make a micro-budget science fiction film, but I advise against attempting anything that is going to be too heavy on the elements mentioned earlier. So, what does that leave you with? A story.

Darren Aronofsky's conceptually dense and technically raw debut Pi (1998) had a budget of $60,000 and Gareth Edwards' narratively rich and technically inventive Monsters (2010) cost $15,000. Both films are distinguished by their stories.

It is really hard to write a chapter on genre considerations in a book on micro-budget screenwriting and not mention Shane Carruth's 2004 Sundance hit Primer. Reportedly made for $7000, the most effective special effect in the time travel story is the dense, highly technical dialogue and concept. Honestly, I could not understand most of what the characters were talking about, but I picked up on the urgency and the drama in the screenplay and got sucked in.

Mike Cahill's Another Earth (2011), also a Sundance hit, was made for $100,000 and lauded for the science elements in the story, but, ultimately, even though the concept underlying the story is clearly science-fiction, the heart of what makes it so effective comes from the characters' dilemma, these are people we care about and invest in. Similarly, Jim Byrkit's Coherence was shot in five days for $50,000. It is completely character and concept driven, a riveting thriller that draws its tension from the interpersonal dynamics among a group of people trapped in a house during a crisis caused by a passing comet. So, you can make a cool science-fiction film, but it is going to require a strong concept to distract audiences from the fact that they are probably not going to see spaceships zooming through the galaxy.

I would be hesitant to approach a western on a budget of $100,000 or less, but it can be done if you have non-budget resources in place. Chloe Zhao's The Rider (2017) was modestly budgeted and benefited considerably by featuring a real cowboy, a guy who, among other things, trains horses for a living as her main character. Since Zhao was shooting in documentary/verite-hybrid style, she was able to shoot his work with the horses. There have been a few other low-budget westerns in recent years, but they tend to be smaller, intimate character-driven stories.

Similarly, if you want to shoot a war film, you are going to have to get especially crafty in your screenplay. It is unlikely that you will be able to stage epic scenes with a large cast, use tanks, bombers, gunfire and explosions. That said, with creative sound design and minimal

CGI, you can suggest a battle going on around your characters. One really handy tip is to, if applicable, connect with re-enactors. These guys come with their own (usually accurately detailed) wardrobe and weapons and, in my experience, often gravitate toward any opportunity to strut their stuff—meaning that you can sometimes luck into getting a bunch of them inexpensively. Years ago, one of my students made a WWI film for his senior thesis (in German, no less) and made extensive use of re-enactors. Lovinder Gill told me about a Civil War film that he wants to make where the bulk of the film involved a young character eager to take up arms. Most of the film would have shown the character traveling on his own to join the army only to discover the bloody aftermath of a battle. Yes, it would have cost something to cast a bunch of re-enactors to play bloody, dead or wounded soldiers, but, for one scene in a film, shot creatively to make the scope of the scene much bigger than it really was, it would probably have been worth it.

Period films are heavily reliant on wardrobes, sets and locations devoid of glaringly obvious contemporary details. If you know that you have access to a period wardrobe and a location largely untouched by time, you might already be thinking about making a film set in another era. Honestly, when I first saw Whit Stillman's Metropolitan (1990), which is set "not so long ago," I did not know that it was supposed to be set in the 1960s. On his modest budget, he could not afford period recreations, so he went in the other direction and attempted to remove all traces of the modern world. Because the film is about upper-class characters participating in decades-old high society functions and rituals, it seemed natural for the actors to be clothed in classic (i.e., timeless) formal wear.

Mickey Keating's black and white psychological thriller Darling (2015) has a timeless look, thanks to wardrobe and lack of cell phones, clearly inspired by films like Polanski's Repulsion (1965) and, for that matter, The Tenant (1976). So, when does it take place? It is hard to tell until a single blink-and-you-won't notice it (the date on the driver's license) gives us a clue.

David Robert Mitchell plays with period in his first feature The Myth of the American Sleepover (2010), $50,000 and, to some

degree, in the follow-up It Follows (2014). There are no comput-
ers in sight, people do not use cell phones but some of them use
e-readers and teenagers watch movies on VHS.

Again, not to belabor the point, the inspiration for a film often
comes from recognizing available elements and concocting a story
that utilizes them.

Polly Schattel offered:

> To do a low budget film, again, you have to use what you have
> available. So contemporary, often rural, because, if you're in
> New York City, it's hard to rent space for no money. You can't
> do a period film because you can't put Model T's on the curb
> outside the general store.

I would be hesitant to suggest making an action film on a micro-
budget unless you happen to know a lot of stunt-savvy actors and fight
coordinators. Yes, of course, Robert Rodriguez pulled it off in the
$7000.00 El Mariachi (1992), but he really knew what he was doing,
really worked within the parameters of what he was capable of, what he
could pull off with a mix of resources at hand, confidence and bravado.

I would advise against car chases if possible because 1) they can be
dangerous even if you do happen to have a stunt driver and 2) they
can be complicated and time-consuming to shoot. Still, as mentioned
elsewhere in this book, I once challenged myself to see if I could write
a $50,000 action film. The entire story takes place in and around a strip
club—the actual bar area, the dressing rooms, the offices, the base-
ment and the parking lot—all one building. It worked. The punchline
here is that, after a producer asked to see it, he told me that he liked
it, wanted to make it but asked me to rewrite it for a $60,000,000
budget. It was fun to blow up the proportions of the story and, as
I recall, blow up some other things in the new version of the story, but
it never got made. Of all of the unmade shards of projects I have sitting
around, this is the one that I keep coming back to, sniffing around and
thinking about making—the original $50,000 version.

Thrillers and, to some extent, crime/gangster films are frequently
a good bet because they are generally driven by complex stories and

characters, both of which might be harder than average to write but cost about the same as simple stories and generic characters. Like the classic film noir canon, thrillers tend to be more about people in situations and less centered on having many locations. Yes, Karyn Kusama's brilliant The Invitation (2015) cost about $1,000,000 to make, but there are few reasons that the story could not have been made at a fraction of the cost in a cheaper location, with less refined production design by less experienced filmmakers and actors—with a screenplay as good as Phil Hay and Matt Manfredi's is. Similarly, Creep (2015) might have been more than $100,000 but that is because, between them, Mark Duplass and Jason Blum could afford to produce it for more. At the heart of it, the story is still Micro Budget friendly.

On an intellectual level, comedy seems to make sense for a micro-budget production, but humor tastes vary and, for whatever it is worth, they tend not to play as well internationally. So, there are lots of small-scale comedies that involve a handful of characters in funny situations. It is a good model to consider but only if you have a screenplay that is widely accessible and funny to anyone who did not work on the film. Kevin Smith's classic Clerks (1994) is famous for its minuscule budget, but it is also a genuinely funny screenplay. Micro-budget romantic comedies and, for that matter, dramas also fit into this category.

I have already mentioned the lower budget musicals Guy and Madeline on a Park Bench (2009) by Damien Chazzelle and Once (2007) by John Carney elsewhere, but it is worth bringing them up again. We tend to think of lavish song and dance sequences in musicals, and it is going to take a lot of effort to pull off this kind of scene on a micro-budget, but, if you have a relationship with a musician who can write and record songs for you at a bargain rate and you are savvy about staging, I would not rule out making a musical although you will likely be limiting yourself to fans of musicals. Because I know a lot of musicians, I have long toyed with the idea of doing an open-mic, aspiring musician-centric story. As mentioned elsewhere in this book, I was once hired to write a micro-budget musical and kept it small in scale by rooting it in the reality of the everyday world and, of course, limiting locations, which, of course, leads us to horror. I like to call horror "the genre that never dies" because it never goes out of style. The horror audience is large, loyal and, with all due respect, not too discriminating. By that I mean the audience tends to be more forgiving of lower production values, amateurish acting, borderline special effects and rehashing overly familiar stories. Basically, as long as there are a reasonable number of scares and, much of the time, lots of gore, many horror fans are satisfied. At the American Film Market, I learned that—big surprise—horror films are the top-selling films. Recalling Dov S-S Simens parting words "Rent a house for the weekend, get a bunch of kids and chop 'em up." Honestly, I sort of feel like I am catching a break when I get hired to write a horror film because they rarely involve Three-Act Structure or character development in the conventional sense; characters do not necessarily have to grow and change; they have to either live or die.

That said, we have been in a new golden age of artsy, intellectual horror films and, as a horror fan myself, I do appreciate them, films like Robert Eggers The Witch (2015) and Trey Edward Shults It Comes At Night (2017)—which was marketed as a horror film but is more of a psychological thriller even though I sat in the theater watching it and actually said to myself "This is truly horrifying." So, in some ways, the bar is high if you are aiming for something beyond the run-of-the-mill horror and yet, plenty of people are simply ignoring that high bar and continuing to crank out basic slice and dice, blood-soaked scary movies.

For a great, easily digestible analysis of the financial considerations surrounding horror movies, check out the short horror movie video produced by NPR's Planet Money.

No matter what genre you choose to work in, if you are proceeding with a micro-budget approach, you will do yourself a big favor by making sure to be well-versed in genre conventions and audience expectations because one way to make your film stand out is by successfully challenging or subverting those conventions and expectations. Few things jump out as "original" more than appearing to give the audience what they want and then pulling off a surprise twist on the genre.

# 8
# CASE STUDIES

In this chapter, the filmmakers I interviewed talked about some of the specific ways that they approached their films.

BOB BYINGTON ON FRANCES FERGUSON (2019): We sort of built the scripts around the woman who plays the lead. And I had workshopped an idea I had for a short with her and then determined that we were trying to make the feature with her. And so we built a story around her personality. Logistically, we knew that we wanted to be in a small town where we would have free reign. The story is also built with North Platte in mind and some of the things you see in the story were built into the script.

MARTHA STEPHENS: Like, Aaron (Katz), I made my first movie in and around my hometown, so I could call in favors, you know, get my cousin to donate our dinner one night. With no money, I was having to put people up in my aunt's house. So I think writing something for where you're from or someplace where you have some kind of a foundation or resources is really smart. You can make that money go a lot further that way.

DOI: 10.4324/9781003138969-9

DG:   I want to go back to the genesis of the project. Did you have the sense of wanting to make a film but knowing that you might not have the financing for a big elaborate film?

JIM BYRKIT:   Totally. There's the sense of sitting down thinking, alright, "I don't have anything. What can I make with nothing?" The main thing is to find something that absolutely inspires you, so that you can't wait to do it. Like for me, I had been working on these big movies that took so long to get one shot off, because you're waiting for the lights, you're waiting for the actors, you're waiting for all the production to happen. And so I had this crazy idea of like, what if I got rid of the two things that really slow me down, which is the script and the crew? And then I could really make a movie? And so I'd been fantasizing about that. Like, what would that look like if I just didn't have a crew? How small could it be? And I thought, well, I do need a DP. And I need sound. You just have to have good sound. And so our crew was me, my DP, Nick Sadler, and two sound guys. And then I couldn't wait to test. It was really an experiment, the whole thing started as an experiment to see what would happen. If, instead of writing out every line of dialogue, I just prepped the characters with their backstory and their relationships.

JB:   It was a 12-page outline just for me, that didn't share it with any-body. It was right for me only so that I could understand what had to happen before the next thing could happen. And I kind of brainstormed it with Alex Manoogian, who plays Amir in the film. And so we would talk about it. And that's how we got to the point of multiple realities. And we would discuss Alright, well, how are these characters in conflict with themselves, everybody has some kind of internal conflict, everybody has a deep relation-ship with the other people. So it becomes this math problem that you really have to talk through over and over and over, in order to give just the tiniest clues to the actors, because the actors are just getting notes every day from me. I've emailed them a few lines or a little story or something. But they wouldn't know what was going to happen. They had no idea, you know what the story was. So we looked at it as almost like a fun house. When you're in a fun house, there's only one door in and out of each room. But you can do whatever you want in the room, you can stay as long as you want, you can look around. But there's one way out of that room. And that's how we looked at the scenes. We don't care what you do in the scene is sort of how I approached it, as long as we hit this, and this and this. And that can trigger the next scene.

DG: I just feel like in a film, this scale, where we don't have set pieces and multiple locations to work with, we have to turn up the heat on those relationships.

JB: Yeah. For something like this, it can't all just be a concept. It can't just be reality fracturing at some point, the human brain first, maybe it's because of the way we evolved, but we're fascinated by human relationships. Our minds can't help but we want to track Okay, who's with who, who likes who who's trying to steal whose boyfriend, right? That's why even in Shakespeare, you know, the Best Writing in the world, there still has these soap opera elements to it, there still has, you know, just very heightened, very well written interpersonal drama. Right. And that because we're human beings, and that's ultimately what we're genetically programmed to care about.

DG: From a writing perspective, did you map that out with every character's relationship with every other character?

JB: Yeah, every character's starting relationship with every character like "you were her teacher. Many years ago, she was your favorite student. Now you become best friends. Even when you were dating this person", like we just talked about that, worked it all out. So everybody knew their history.

DG: So you left certain elements of the story, for lack of a better phrase, open ended.

JB: Oh, for sure. I think about all the characters, clearly having interpersonal dynamics between each one, and that gets really mathy. In terms of relationships and because I wanted the surprise, I wanted the collaboration to work with great actors, because they have so much to bring in. If you've just already scripted every single word, then all they're doing is a variation of those words. But this was much more fun, because I would give them prompts, and then see where they take it. Like, I had no idea that the interpersonal conflicts at the table would sort of generate so much tension when Laurie is confused about seeing Mike in her favorite TV show. That was originally just supposed to be a commentary on another version of him. You know, he's, he's an actor, and there's another version of him out there. But to see it sort of escalate to this really weird metaphysical battle and challenge and challenge to his ego, and then how he had to respond by insulting her memory. That was just gold. And that's when, as a filmmaker, you're holding the camera, you're so excited. You're just hoping for your focus, because it's magic.

DG: You shot this in a week or something like that.

JB: Five Nights, five hours a night.

---

TOM QUINN: On The New Year Parade, you go and you meet people, you hear how they talk, and then you come back and you're writing that. And if I build trust, that's a thing that will add specificity and value, and all kinds of visuals to my film. That, to me, is part of the writing process. I do think like that, like research and like relationship building can really be part of the process in a way that is even more on a Micro Budget, or at least in a different way on a Micro Budget than you would if you were like writing a script and then turned over to production in another way. Because it's building you the things that are going to save you money later. But also adding specificity to your scripts that sort of beyond what you do have access to. On The New Year Parade, I would do that and I would write drafts of the script. And then I put scenes up on this Mummers message board and they would shred it and then they would be like, "We would never say." They would just make fun of it but, weirdly, it made them start to like me, because they knew I wasn't just like, writing a thing that they were gonna be embarrassed of. But since I could hang in there a little bit, they started to like me, and then when we would meet in person later on in production, we had trust.

So on The New Year Parade, it was a pretty traditional 100, 105 maybe 110 not 120 page script or something. And, then we would rehearse that quite a bit. And I would ask Jen, who played Kat, if there are scenes that you think are missing, as someone who's gone through a similar situation, tell me what they are and we can write them. And so, I had done the eight drafts in a very traditional way first. And then it's interesting because we almost never looked at the script in production but we would use it from a breakdown standpoint. And, but then we would do long, like 20 minute, takes that were kind of improv. If we ever got stuck, they go back to the script, and they say the lines and usually what that would get me by the end was a mix of what I had written, and a mix of what they came up with and I could kind of dial that back and forth in the edit.

RY RUSSO-YOUNG: I literally reunited with someone that I went to high school with, my best friend's younger sister and I just started interviewing her as a character and we kind of made up the character as she went along. And I was just asking the character questions and we shot a three-hour interview and I found her fascinating as a character and then we had some friends come over and we shot some like verite scenes with her in character and the other friends were kind of playing characters and kind of playing themselves. Then I went home and I edited this footage and I looked at it and I showed it to some friends and I said "Is this interesting? I think this is fascinating. Like she's a really interesting character, right? Like, don't you agree? Yes, no, am I crazy?" And they all said "Yes, this is really interesting. Keep going with it." So I started just writing out little scenes that I wanted to see the character in that felt right for the choices we had already made for her. So they would improvise the scenes I didn't even write dialogue in.

LAWRENCE MICHAEL LEVINE: But anything that I've done myself, I've written for myself, I've done with a mind to giving costs as low as possible. Because I always wanted to be able to say "Okay, well, if I can't raise my money outside, I can always just find a way to pay for it myself."

But from a writing perspective, it started with just trying to keep things interesting, with as few characters in as few locations as possible. This is just what I've done with every movie that I've written, including Black Bear, with the mindset of keeping costs down. Gabi On The Roof In July (2010) was written less with price in mind than almost any of my other movies. And I don't really exactly know why. I mean, it was just such a wild, crazy process. We made Gabi On The Roof In July for about, I don't know, $38,000 and then we made Always Shine (2016) for maybe $100,000.

It is hard to get people's attention and say something meaningful in a two-hour window. And that's what, that's what making movies is, it doesn't matter if you're relying on special effects. Or if you're lying on interpersonal dynamics, you have to have something to say, and it has to be interesting. It's kind of like movies now, or in the same thing as rock or it's, or country music or whatever, three chords, and the truth is just like, you got a camera and the truth, you can make a movie.

So the question is, like, how do you get to the truth? And in my case, it just was a lot of learning how to write, spending a lot of time writing and studying, studying people who had done what I wanted to do. So, you know, after I had done this play, the technology came out and existed where you could shoot something and edit it in your house and I took advantage of it. And that was my first film (Territory), and then the next film Gabi On The Roof In July. It's interesting, because that was when I got involved with Sophia, romantically and creatively. And she's such an incredible organizer and producer, that I, at that point, in a way kind of abdicated those kinds of responsibilities and thought to myself, well, we're gonna make something and she's going to figure out how to do this, you know? In fact, almost more than any of my other films I didn't really think, think consciously about keeping things cheap. With Territory, my first thing, I knew three-people-one-location that it was going to be cheap. But Gabi was many characters, many locations. I think I had been emboldened by watching some of my contemporaries like Andrew Bujalski and Swanberg. You know, and people like that. I think those were the two big ones at the time. And I was like, "these guys are making movies where people are all over the place. So obviously, it can be done. I'll just, I'll shoot in my apartment, I'll shoot in my friend's apartment, we'll get permits for the street," which I learned from film school that you could do. And so I kind of moved out of that three- people-one-location mindset and was like, "No, you can do this with lots of different people." In a way, I feel like, of all of the stuff that people call mumblecore, Gabi is almost Altman-esque and it's kind of because it has a lot of characters and a lot of locations and stuff. It has more characters.

So, it was a great experience in that way. I think the plan was that we were going to do about six months of rehearsals, we're going to make up the characters together and we were going to make up the story together. And then it was like, and then we were going to start to film the rehearsals. I came up with a lot of character questions and there was good preparation for that, because then all this character development I did in tandem with the actors. It was a character quiz and a character questionnaire that I gave everybody. And it was really cool. I mean, I think they really felt ownership of their roles and their characters. And they were really engaged with the project because of it. Basically, Sophia, and I transcribed all of those rehearsals. So we had like 300 pages of material that we whittled down to about 160. But it was very collaborative, because a lot of the dialogue was generated by the actors themselves. Then Sophia helped me and Kate Kurtz, another screenwriter, helped me in terms of figuring out what went into the movie and what went out. It wasn't like any other script writing process I've ever been involved in where, you know, basically, I'm alone, and I devise everything myself. And there's nobody else really involved except some people who gave me notes. This was a totally collaborative effort. I did my own final pass the week before the week before the shoot. So Sophia was like, "Get this thing as short as you can, until the week before the shoot, then go off and figure out how you're going to shoot this movie and do a final pass on the script." And that's pretty much exactly what happened. But when we started the shoot, the script was 162 pages, which is long. And what happened was, after we shot this week that then had to be completely reshot. I, once again, had to look at the script with Sophia and Kate. And we had to rewrite it. We had to be like, "Okay, what can say what can go because now we can't afford, we don't have time, we can't afford to shoot this scene, we had a big scene like in an AA meeting, we would have required extras and additional location to shoot", so we had to cut that out. So, after we had to reshoot this entire week, I had to go back and cut a bunch of scenes and alter the story significantly. And, and what you see is the final movie as a result of that. So that's kind of a crazy process. And I've never done anything like that, again, although I'd be interested in it. It required a lot of things. And also feeling like I had nothing to lose, feeling like it might be fun to revisit that process. Again, you know, many years later. I think it'd be nice to like, go back and revisit those characters and do something with all the same cast.

In some ways, Black Bear is my most contained film that I've made since territory.

It's mainly three characters; half of it is three characters in one location. And then it's like maybe 10–12 characters in one location, but it's all set in one location. You know, I think the focus needs to be on character's motivation when you can't rely on external conflict, special effects or action. You know, whatever normal movies tend to do, it just really comes down to character, their predicament and the relatability of their predicaments and then drawing people in based on characters.

On Green (2011), we wanted to do it even cheaper because we had just lost our lunch with Gabi. It was financed by Sophia, who had been cast in a commercial that she was ultimately basically cut out of. I think you see her for a second.

Sophia wrote an outline. The location was Sophia's dad's country house. And then (actress) Kate Lyn Sheil, myself and Sophia improvise the scenes. And then they started to take shape. And then I think there was some rewriting that went on in between the two shoots, because that was done, like I said, in two parts, one in which we shot and failed. And the second which we shot and I guess, succeeded.

---

NOAM KROLL: Probably the greatest challenge, I would say, just from a visual standpoint, trying to write for those locations was tricky because, although I think both locations looked good and I knew where I was going to shoot even during the rewriting phase so I could actually, you know, sort of write with that in mind. Um, and although I thought they looked great on camera, both locations were really small. For example, the second location we filmed in, I knew we were supposed to show three bedrooms, but there were only two bedrooms in the actual house. So right away there were those sort of challenges as I was writing. I was trying to stay conscious and cognizant of the physical parameters that we would be in. And, and, you know, to some extent that was helpful because it allowed me to sort of visualize how the scene would play out. But, in other ways, it was challenging because, when you're writing a script and you don't have to worry about "if I write the character walking out onto the balcony, does this house actually have a balcony?" Usually you don't worry about that, you just write it and if there's no balcony, you rewrite it and that's it. But in this case I knew. So that sort of almost created a bit of a writer's block kind of in certain moments where I would try to get through scenes and then get stuck because I'd realize "What's the point in writing the scene if it's going to have to change, or if that location is going to work?" So, that was definitely an issue.

So in my first feature film, Shadows On The Road (2018), just to contrast that film with Psychosynthesis, every day, we were in a different location and I didn't even have to worry about the visuals. You know, one day we're on the beach the next day, where, you know, in the desert and everyday it was something else. So that was sort of baked into the idea for the purpose of it, not becoming stale and still feeling like the story was progressing and the mood was progressing. And in this case, I didn't have that crutch to lean on because we were only in the two locations. So it really forced me to sort of lean into those scene descriptions and those visuals on the page in a way that hopefully would differentiate things and keep it all fresh.

NK:   I wrote this film knowing it would probably wind up at 70 something-thing minutes, but actually I think the script was over 90. Maybe it was 89 pages or 90 pages or something. So, quite a bit was cut from it. But I think that's actually an important point for filmmakers to remember, especially if they've never made a feature before, is that what happens if you really go through the editorial process is at a certain point, you have to become ruthless with the material and you start cutting stuff left. And right. So if you're starting with an 85 page script or in this case, let's say someone sees a movie like mine and they say, "Oh, cool. I want to make a 70 minute movie." Don't write a 70 page script necessarily because then you have no room.

DG:   Did you feel that the 100 minute cut wasn't working?

NK:   Yeah, I didn't think it worked as well. I think there were scenes in there that were fine, but they didn't progress the story the way that I intended, they didn't capture the mood. Maybe there was something that we explored that we improvised in a scene that covered an element. So there might be this five minute or three minute scene, let's say, and there was really only one line in that theme that actually mattered. So we would just cut that scene. And in some cases I would be in the edit, take a line and put it in the background or sneak it into another part of the story. But, yeah, it was just too much material. And I think no matter what, there's always the case. I mean, anyone, even on big studio movies, they have a 130 page script and then the first cut ends up being three and a half hours. And then by the time they're done, it's an hour and 50. So you want to have a, you want to give yourself wiggle room when you're writing and, and build in some, some extra breathing space. So you can give yourself those puzzle pieces later on and figure out which ones fit and which ones don't.

DG: Did you accommodate for budget limitations in the screenplay? Did you, for instance, write in locations that you knew you would have access to? That kind of thing?

ANGELA MARIE HUTCHINSON: I definitely looked at, "Okay, what locations do we have accessible?" As an example, with a basketball player character, for example, I remember when we were actually mapping out all of our days, and all of our shooting days were like, "Gosh, are we actually going to be able to get to a basketball court, for these two actors to go shoot scenes?" Are we really going to go to a park, or we're going to send like a remote crew over to go do this while we're shooting something else? And then we're like, "Let's just change them from playing basketball to them working out in a gym, which we could shoot at our current location, and so, they were just lifting weights, doing the same lines that they would have been saying on the basketball court."

ROBERT GREENE: The title Kate Plays Christine literally comes from me thinking about Kate Lyn Sheil playing the role. Like there was no other choice. There was no casting process. It was Kate. I called her and I said, "Hey, I got an idea. Do you want to do this? It's literally this." And the film, for all the twists and turns that we went through, became almost exactly the film that we talked about on the phone that day. And that's because of the concept and the script. And the or the concept in the scripting, I would say not the script, because it was those scripts, the concept of the scripting, and the execution and the pursuit of it were all intertwined. And that's because we only had so much money, we only had so much time, we had to make it work.

For his film Drinking Buddies (2013), like all of his films, Joe Swanberg employed what he calls a "scriptment," no dialogue but long descriptions of emotional beats and action. The scriptment for the 90 minute film was 45 pages of extensive notes on what happens in each scene. Swanberg famously casts actors who are adept at improvising dialogue but he is not just setting them up in front of a camera and telling them to speak. Before stepping in front of the camera, they have been given lots of information on who the character is, what he or she wants, what the obstacles are and what attempts to overcome them should or should not be in the scene. A few years ago, I had Swanberg as a guest speaker in one of my screenwriting classes. He leaned over to me before starting and said "I'm not really sure what to talk about since I have never written a screenplay." When we turned on the projector and were able to take a look at one of his scriptments, I said to him "That's a screenplay." Anyone taking a look at that document would have been able to understand what needed to be produced. In fact, we looked through the pages describing the opening sequence of an episode of his Netflix series Easy. Then we watched the sequence and it was exactly as described. That is, in part, screenwriting.

ALEX ROSS PERRY "Every problem that I knew would come up from having gone to film school and made an overly expensive, unnecessary thesis, I was solving because I said, "I'm going to make a movie. The thesis shoot was eight days and I said, I'm going to shoot a feature in less days than that for less money. And it's going to be three times as long, I'm going to shoot a 70 minute movie for the same $20,000 or less. We're not going to do it like a student film; a professional schedule where you do maybe two or three pages a day, we're gonna do this the way people my age are now doing this, where you're shooting like 10 or 15 minutes of usable footage a day. And you're shooting for seven days. You know, that's still plenty of material, I think, a movie 73 minutes long, I think I probably shot maybe four and a half hours for it, you know, 30 minutes a day for seven days, roughly."

DG: So, you were making the story up as you were shooting?
NIGEL BACH: I had to write down ideas about what it would be so it wasn't a script, per se, it became an outline that I operated off

of. And, like, there were times where it was reverse engineering, when I found somebody that wanted to be in it, I would create a situation. In the case where I'm the only actor in the film, I have to only remember what I'm supposed to do, but when I involve other people in it, I can't think that they're inside my head to know everything so that's why I wrote out a screenplay for Badder Ben (2017) and for Steelmanville Road (2017), and for the Crescent Moon Clown (2018).

I knew you'd written many screenplays and your Badder Ben co-stars Matthew Schmidt and Jacquie Baker had written sketches and I could have gotten the same result, but it would have taken five times as long five times as five times as long if I had just said, "This is what I want to happen, adlib." And it was more efficient to write out a screenplay and present it to you guys. But what I find by doing that is my actors are more dependent on a script in the beginning and then they begin to take ownership of the character and then they become the character by the last third of the movie. And they are able to rely less on a screenplay and more on what the person they're representing and what their character would do in that situation.

---

VERA BRUNNER-SUNG: Bella Vista sort of came to me and we made it happen in a relatively quick turnaround, the shoot was like 12 days. I think the script was 45 pages but I thought it would probably be between 75 and 85, maybe 90 minutes long. But I realized, with a feature, that you will reach more people than you will with an experimental short film, even the most experimental feature is probably going to reach more people. I felt like I was doing something bigger and more different and more ambitious than anything I'd ever done before, relative to my body of work and it was a real opportunity in terms of pushing me to think bigger. I'm working on things that feel much bigger and more ambitious and more, you know. I spent several years in development, something that would have seemed insane to me. At that time when I was making Bella Vista, I was like, "Why would anyone spend more than, you know, a year working on their scripts?" Now I'm a better writer and I just have a clear vision of what I want my work to do and I couldn't have gotten to this place without making that film the way that we made it.

# 9
## STOMPING GROUND

One day, in 1988, on the production of Signs of Life in Maine, I body-doubled for actor Vincent D'Onofrio, even though he is about eight inches taller than me. It was one of his first big parts. Years later, D'Onofrio had gone on to become a well-established, well-regarded actor and I was one of the film reviewers for IndieTalk.com and Home Media Entertainment magazine. I found myself reviewing his feature writing-directing debut, a micro-budget horror–musical called Don't Go In The Woods (2010). It is not a very good movie in the conventional sense but I kind of liked it.

I read up about it and even found an interview with him where he said that the plan was to "make a bad horror movie" where they intentionally cast unknowns who had music and singing experience whether or not they had acting experience. He cast a band that his nephew was friends with, he cast some girls who worked at the coffee shop around the corner from him and he cast a couple of girls who had been extras on Law & Order and they shot in 12 days on his property in upstate New York for $100,000.

The whole piece smacks of artistic experimentation, like D'Onofrio, was making a test film and challenging his own notions of what acting and film could be. The clue to this theory is that the film really only ever comes alive during the musical numbers. In general, the songs (written by co-screenwriter Sam Bisbee) are

DOI: 10.4324/9781003138969-10

actually pretty catchy, decent takes on the acoustic indie-rock singer-songwriter vibe that would be right at home playing in the background of a scruffy little coffeehouse. That the cast, made up of enthusiastic, fresh-faced but character-appropriate-grungy 20-somethings, is clearly better at performing the music than they are at delivering lines seems to suggest D'Onofrio picked people with some musical skills who might or might not be able to act rather than casting actors who have some musical skills. The difference might seem subtle on paper and, in action, it jumps out, but the film has a loopy, engaging, infectious "let's put on a show" energy.

So, it seems like D'Onofrio was going for a degree of Neo-realism here a la Vittorio De Sica, Gus Van Sant's Elephant 2003 and Paranoid Park (2007) and Matthew Porterfield's Putty Hill.

In that regard, the experiment pays off to a degree in that, overall, the attractive cast does have an appeal, they really do feel like a social circle plucked off the streets of NYC by someone who wanted to make a film about who they are—fresh, raw and palpably full of spirit, no baggage, giving it their all and probably not for the promise of what, presumably, was not a huge payday.

Sometimes it seems like certain filmmakers are trying to make a point about bad films by going out and making a bad film, almost a sly send-up of bad films. So what is this film, a drama with bad acting, a musical without a good story or a horror film without any scares? The whole thing felt as if it was really about D'Onofrio and some friends getting their feet wet, experimenting with film-making in anticipation of more ambitious projects to come. He went on to write and direct the considerably more polished The Kid (2019) Since this chapter has taken an unexpected detour into a discussion of Vincent D'Onofrio's directing career, it only seems right to mention his only other directing credit Five Minutes, Mr. Welles (2005), a wonderful 30-minute short in which he gives an amazing performance as Orson Welles.

So what did all of this mean for me? Could I, a nobody, throw together a cast/crew of nobodies, run around, shoot a film and throw it up on the Internet? Sure, I guess I could. Did I know that I had screenplays sitting around that were designed to be shot for little-to-no money? Sure did! If I went out and made one, would anyone see it?

Oddly, watching Don't Go In The Woods was one of the things that really inspired me to give Stomping Ground, which had now been optioned twice but did not seem to be going anywhere, a shot.

My screenplay Incorporated had been a semi-finalist to get into the Sundance Screenwriters Lab and, even though I had written it for a relatively low budget, I did not think I could raise enough money to do it justice. I'm not a natural producer and I am not especially good at the fundraising/financing side of things, so, without anyone to partner with, I seriously doubted my ability to pull it off on my own.

So, in 2005, I turned my attention to another, even less expensive project but ran into the same problem. Then I wrote Aftermath, which eventually became Stomping Ground, specifically with the idea that I had to come up with a viable project. I decided to take a scientific approach to writing a screenplay utilizing all of the lessons I learned over the years, to write an innovative, inventive screenplay that could be shot in 1–2 days for little to no money and avoid all the narrative and technical pitfalls that plagued so many micro-budget productions. The film could not merely be cheap; it had to be entertaining and accessible, something that would appeal to both an art-house crowd and a mainstream audience.

I knew that I was not going to be able to raise much money and, because I didn't think I could get a cast and crew to work for free for very long, that it was going to have to be a really short shoot. I also started thinking about ways to shoot it quickly. Because the screenplay is essentially a one-act play that takes place mostly in one location and in real time, I knew that there was a great risk of it becoming static and stagy. In the writing phase, I knew that the standard Three-Act Structure would not suit this story.

Borrowing lessons discussed in Chapter 6, things I learned from teaching my Writing The Short Film courses, the inciting incident in Stomping Ground happens off-screen. The film is about the aftermath of a random act of violence, but the violent act is never shown on screen, it happens before the movie starts, so the story begins in crisis. Also, in a significant break with convention, the inciting incident is not something that happens to the main character, it is something he chooses to do. Similarly, also from the lessons I learned from short films, some things are left unresolved at the end. Sure, there are suggestions of some definitive moments but nothing is spelled out, nobody grows and changes for the better and, inasmuch as there is a good guy, when you really think about it, while he appears to be the voice of reason, the moral compass of the story, in the end, he emerges as someone few would call noble.

I had a colleague for awhile, screenwriter Joe Stinson, who wrote four screenplays for Clint Eastwood (including the iconic line "Go ahead, make my day"), a really sweet guy, but, if he did not like your screenplay, you would hear about it. So, one day, I saw him reading Stomping Ground and I prepared for the worst. When he finished and came over, he said "You managed to break all of the rules of screenwriting and still come up with a piece that works."

With Stomping Ground, I knew that I could not have a 20-minute stretch where nothing major happens, so I made sure to write in major act breaks, revelations, complications or decisions every seven to ten pages. Knowing that watching four guys in the woods could get old really fast, I knew that I had to keep my foot on the drama pedal, keep throwing things at the characters to keep the audience engaged or, at least, distracted from the reality that they were just four guys in the woods shot with low production values.

Now, while the focus of this book is on screenwriting because there are plenty of other books on micro-budget production, I did write with the shooting style in mind. From a technical standpoint, one of the best ways of keeping your film from being static and stagy is to avoid having your camera be locked down. No, I am not the biggest fan of shaky handheld camerawork, but I knew I was going to have to employ it.

Next, because of my background in theater and my experience with film production, I came upon the idea to shoot Stomping Ground as if I had been hired to shoot a play. You would never go into a theater, set up a camera in the back and just get one wide, static shot of the stage. Well, I guess that, if you have kids and they have ever done anything on stage, maybe you would shoot it in that fashion. If I had a gig shooting a stage performance, I would do my best to show up to the theater with at least three or four cameras and set them up around the room. So, that's how I decided to shoot my film, as if it was a one-act play being shot by three to four handheld cameras almost always in motion. The actors would know all of their lines, not just the ones being shot that day as most films are shot. Cameras would roll, I would call "action," the actors would do the screenplay start to finish, I'd yell "cut," we would take a break and do it a few more times.

I have to admit that, for better or worse, I got caught up with the idea of shooting a feature in 24 hours and breaking so many of the rules of screenwriting. I had to put my theory to the test.

In the summer of 2006, I had assembled a cast and crew but, just hours before the first day of the shoot, my lead actor quit due to personal reasons. I rescheduled the shoot for a couple of months later, the lead actor came back and, the night before the first day of shooting, he broke his foot and then moved to L.A. I recast the whole film, scrambled to replace the original crew and it just never came together.

All along, a producer in L.A. had been asking me to option the screenplay and I had been turning her down. I optioned it to a Philly company, it never really progressed, the producer in L.A. asked about optioning it again and the third time was the charm. I sold the rights to the screenplay for two years and was hired to rewrite it for six months. Near the end of the two-year option, the producer stopped responding to calls and emails. It often turns out that, if neither party takes action at the end of an option, the producer can sometimes retain the rights for free. With about two weeks to spare and the help of a generous volunteer lawyer, I retained the rights to my screenplay. That was in January 2011.

On July 1, 2013, I met with a bright, daring, ambitious young producer and we decided to go ahead with my idea that Stomping Ground could be shot in two days. I kept waiting for someone to say "Okay, Dave, we're not really going to shoot it in two days, right?" We mounted an aggressive crowd-funding campaign that brought in a big chunk of our budget. I have to come clean about one of the more successful elements of the crowd-funding campaign. As it was drawing to a close and looking like it might fall short of our goal, I went on social media and posted "Thank you Kevin Smith! Thank you Edward Burns!" suggesting that these two icons of micro-budget filmmaking had become aware of the campaign and contributed. What more needs to be said about the power of suggestion? I never said that they contributed but people interpreted it that way and we got a surge of new backers. Still, the campaign was going to fall short, so one of the producers and I each kicked in enough to put us over the top. It is really important to point out that the production of Stomping Ground depended heavily on the cast building rapport and knowing all of their lines before the shoot, so we rehearsed extensively for a month before hitting the location. It is also important to note that my theoretical approach to the production, having the cast perform the screenplay start to finish, in real time, while we shot did not work. After shooting the first scene or two, we realized that this approach was not going to work. My industrious producers broke down the screenplay, rescheduled the shoot in a ridiculously short amount of time and we got right back to business, barely missing a beat. While my original approach to the production did not work in practice, we still shot it in two 12-hour days and wrapped it on September 1, 2013.

After two and a half draining, demanding, arduous years of post-production, Stomping Ground was completed in January 2016 and premiered in May at the Philadelphia Independent Film Festival.

From the start, I knew the film was going to be divisive, mostly because of the way I planned to shoot it and partly because of the story. I wanted to test a theory that a bad screenplay produced well would probably result in a bad film, but that a good screenplay produced badly might still yield a good film. I wanted to strip everything away so that all I was left with was a good story and good acting.

Stomping Ground is a sloppy film. I always knew it would be. I wanted it to be. Before I even wrote the screenplay, I told myself "I pity the editor who, one day, will have to make sense of this mess." My editor, Robert Larkin worked wonders with the footage we gave him, and it is as choppy and hand-held as I expected it to be. I shot the film in 24 hours in part because I knew I would not be able to afford the cast and crew for much longer and I also thought it might make for good P.R. If I had it to do over again, I would have shot it in 36 hours.

Making Stomping Ground was pretty tough. Everyone tells you that it can be brutal to make a film, that it can push you to the limits of any number of things. I remember, one night, I was leaving the recording studio in the suburbs where we were doing the sound effects and music and then driving downtown to work with the colorist and I was so stressed that I was saying to myself "Never again! I will never put myself through this and make another film!" Was I serious? Was I kidding myself?

Godard's Breathless (1960) is a sloppy, choppy, anarchistic film, and I feel like almost every great film since 1960 owes it a debt of respect. Okay, maybe that is extreme and I, in no way, want to be seen as comparing my film to it. But I was inspired as heck by it. I call Breathless cinematic punk rock. Much like the music that emerged as a response to political strife and bloated corporate music of the 1970s, in 1960, Breathless was a bold and brash reaction to the bloated films coming out of the Hollywood machine, and it really shook things up, much like, decades later, the way Nirvana shook up a music industry that was, once again, in need of some shaking up. Still, I was a shy, sensitive, nerdy tween in the 1970s, but I followed the exploits of the Sex Pistols et al. the way some people watch the stock market. That said, I had an uneasy relationship with punk rock because I was a generally happy, well-adjusted kid who did not have that much to rebel against. I liked a lot of the music and the esthetic but never felt like dressing the part because, at the end of the day, I am a basically nice guy, I am not a punk and, not to call out my many well-adjusted peers and contemporaries who did embrace it, literally wearing it on their sleeves, for me to pretend that I was mad at the world or somehow dangerous or something, just felt disingenuous. Stomping Ground, however, is what I call a "punk rock production," because I was so sick of seeing bad, bloated, ridiculously expensive films devoid of heart and soul. I wanted to be sincere, to explore platonic love among young men who are aware that they probably have emotions but are not always adept at managing them. Like punk rock, I wanted the emphasis to be on characters and story rather than technical proficiency. I always wanted to tell a sad, angry story with something to say about sad, angry people.

Stomping Ground was submitted to quite a few film festivals and has not been accepted by that many. Bottom–line, I have sat in screenings with filmmakers, film lovers and film students who cannot see past the technical flaws. I have seen it with "civilians," regular folks who just want to sit down to watch a movie and I have heard them gasp, laugh, exclaim "Oh my God!" and I have seen them on the edge of their seats.

I knew what I was getting into when I started to make Stomping Ground. I knew that it might be one of those films that never got distribution—either because it was so bad or because there was nobody to champion it. I always thought Stomping Ground would find an audience. It has not, yet.

Remember that most of us make films or want to make films because we love films. That said, even when we use the term "Micro Budget," we are talking about money and nobody wants to lose money. I lost money on Stomping Ground, my own money. No, you do not have to pander to the audience, but, depending on your aspirations, you need to be conscious of the market. The wider the appeal of your film, the more likely it is to attract a bigger paying audience. I say, write from your heart, do what you feel, but if that approach leads you to an obtuse subject matter, you have to know that you are likely aiming for a small, niche target audience and, sad as it is to say, you might need to ask yourself if the investment, however small, will be worth the limited return on investment.

Did I achieve the cinematic acclaim and notoriety I so desperately craved? Not yet. Will I ever? Not counting on it.

Am I disappointed? Sure. Defeated? Not exactly. I actually see the Amazon release as a fresh opportunity to get the film out there and part of me just wishes that I had completely sidestepped the festival submission route in the first place. Has it gotten lots of negative reviews? You bet. Has it gotten a handful of glowing reviews? Yup. That is the risk of trying to make art.

One of the biggest surprises over the course of this whole experience has been the number of close friends and associates who seem to think I cannot handle negative criticism. So many people have asked to see the film, gotten it and never offered me any feedback, as if it simply never happened. I know that they probably do not want to hurt my feelings and I get it, but sometimes no response is worse than a negative response. Of course, not everyone wants to offer an unsolicited critique. I made the mistake of giving a friend some unsolicited but respectful notes on his film after seeing it at a festival in 2012. We have not spoken since.

I feel like I successfully accomplished what I set out to do from the beginning, not pander to conventions, not accommodate for a lack of story by covering it up with state-of-the-art graphic effects but delivering a good, rich, important story performed well by my talented cast.

You can see Stomping Ground on Amazon now. If you like it and have something nice to say, I'd appreciate a positive review. If you see and do not like it, feel free to write a negative review.

It's not enough to make a film these days, anyone can make a film, that's only half the battle—not even half. Getting people to see your film is the trick.

There are so many immaculately produced, state-of-the-art films out there that have unconvincing stories. What is the point of making a film if it does not have a compelling, believable, provocative story? The average cost of a major Hollywood film is somewhere around $80,000,000 and, of that number, the screenplay represents a tiny fraction, usually no more than a few million dollars, but, to me, it is the essential ingredient. I am not saying that screenwriters should be paid more, I am just saying that producers should not make a film until they have an extremely good screenplay. It's not that hard, get a screenplay, ask the writer to do re-writes and, if you're not happy with them, get another screenwriter to make revisions. Importantly, do not call the screenplay finished when you're happy, call it finished when there is a consensus of sound opinions that feel it is a great screenplay.

Stomping Ground is a reaction to people throwing buckets of money at bad screenplays and turning them into beautifully produced bad movies. Stomping Ground was not beautifully produced, it is a ragged, rough around the edges mess but I think it has a good story.

A veteran screenwriter told me that he related to it on a deeply personal level. That's the kind of film I want to make, films that make people say either "I remember when something like this happened to me" or "I can imagine what it would feel like if this happened to me."

In a 2017 New York Times interview, Steven Soderbergh said "It's really easy to make a movie that five people understand. It's really hard to make something that a lot of people understand, and yet is not obvious, still has subtlety and ambiguity, and leaves you with something to do as a viewer."

So, no, Stomping Ground did not make me an "indie darling," did not catapult me to the head of the class, if anything, it might have landed me near the bottom of the waiting list to get into the school. However, when I pitched this book and submitted my proposal, much of the feedback that came back from peer reviewers fell down along the lines of "he is qualified to write this book because he made his own Micro Budget film."

Epilogue: while writing this book, 15 years after writing the screenplay, nine years after shooting the film and five years after finishing it, Stomping Ground got a deal with a well-respected boutique film distributor.

# 10
# FINAL THOUGHTS

For many aspiring screenwriters, the dream is to break into the business by selling their screenplay, getting it produced, then moving onto writing another screenplay and selling it. Remember, as mentioned at the beginning of this book, the reality is that 94% of screenwriting jobs are assignments, paid gigs where you are hired to work on an existing property already in some stage of development. I can tell you that, as a writer for hire, you do not always love the story you are getting paid to write: the job is "take this story and turn it into a screenplay" and, inasmuch as I ever actually make decent money, I take almost every job that comes my way; I cannot afford to be picky—okay, I once turned down a job writing a sequel to a film considered one of the worst ever made. What does seem to be happening is that big producers and studios are looking to independent filmmakers who have written, produced and directed award-winning low-budget films that get distributed.

A director friend of mine recently had a chat with the resident producer at the Independent Feature Project. The producer told my friend that "people in Hollywood want to see if you can take a $70,000 budget and make a film that looks like it was shot for $1,000,000."

The point is that it is no longer enough to pin your hopes to a great screenplay that you can sell, you have to craft a screenplay that

DOI: 10.4324/9781003138969-11

you and some filmmaker friends can actually produce for little-to-no money and the first step in that process is learning specific tricks, hacks and philosophical approach to write screenplays for the type of film.

Screenwriting can be fun. Yes, to do it well and make a living doing it takes a lot of hard work. Until the point where you are doing it for a living, it can be a lot of fun to come up with stories, characters, give them lines and imagine who you would cast in the roles and, to me, it sounds like it could be a fun hobby. That said, I want to caution people about taking this kind of thing too seriously. Remember, in a practical sense, a screenplay really only does anyone any good if they are making a movie. If you are a painter, you can hang your pictures on a wall. If you are a musician, you can play for people. If you are not making it into a movie, what do you do with a screenplay when it is finished?

I once got the question "I have created my own cinematic universe with ten screenplays, how do I sell it to Hollywood?" Sadly, you do not, that is just not the way it works. I do not want to spoil the party or crush anyone's fun, but there is a difference between writing a bunch of screenplays for fun and writing a screenplay that is a viable project from a financial perspective, basically something that investors/stockholders can actually be made into a film that people will want to see.

No lie, I met someone whose plan to support his family was "take Robert McKee's class, write a screenplay and sell it for a million dollars." The spec screenplay market is no longer what it was for a brief time in the 1990s. Sure, out of the 100,000 specs that get sent to Hollywood every year, a few (literally less than 100) get sold and, of those few, now and then, one goes for somewhere in the mid-six figures. At this point, I would find it frustrating to write screenplays for fun; if I write something, I write something that has a good chance of getting produced. By "good chance of getting produced," I mean that it either has marketable qualities that someone in the business might find attractive or that it was written to be produced on a micro-budget.

Be conscious of the business end of things. Keep in mind that most people do not make money on their first feature. I like to think of first features as coming attractions for subsequent work. Make a film, maybe develop a small following of people who will look forward to your next film and the one after that. If you are just looking to get rich, there are probably better ways to go about doing it.

Okay, enough gloom. On the other hand, if you love film, making movies and solving puzzles, maybe writing a micro-budget screenplay is the right way to go. For me, I absolutely love the challenge of writing for micro-budgets; it is a test of both my storytelling—

How do I make this story active and compelling?
But also my knowledge of nuts and bolts film production—

How could we shoot this scene?
Where could we shoot this scene?
How can we cheat this stunt?
How can we keep the narrative and the visuals engaging?

Remember, as mentioned earlier, years ago—for fun, mind you—I challenged myself to write a one-location micro-budget action film. It was, in the end, a lot of fun. A few years later, a producer friend hit me and asked if I had any action screenplays laying around. I said, "Why, yes, I do and it can be made for $50,000!" He said, "Do you think you can rewrite it for a $60,000,000 budget?" I did and it was kind of fun to radically expand it into this big action film where nothing was constrained by budgets—a helicopter chase down the middle of city streets? Sure, why not?

But it was not as much fun as solving the puzzle of setting a whole action film in one location.

All of this stuff gets back to something that I bring up on the first day of class every semester: the role of the artist in society. Artists take in the world, observe and consider some piece of the human experience and then represent (or RE-present) it in some form to an audience. In a best-case scenario, a work of art provokes the audience, stirring emotions and ideas. Either the audience responds and relates to it or reacts against it. We all have different experiences, and we all have different tastes. Yes, you should draw on personal experiences and feelings about things you have seen and done; they should inform your work, but you have to remember to say something about the world other than that it exists.

I remember going to see the feature debut of a legendary television showrunner. The producers of his film clearly took great pains to be extremely accurate about period details, but the film itself was rather flat. The problem is that we do not go to movies to see great production design; we go to see good stories about interesting characters working through circumstances that, in one way or another, we relate to, think about and take something away from, deriving a new sense of the world and our place in it, whether we know it or not.

I tell my students on both the first and the last days of class that, as artists, they need to decide what they want to be and what kind of work they want to do. They should be provocative; that is, create work that not only entertains but also strikes a chord and makes people think or feel something about the world around them, either on a small, intimate, personal level or on a broader, grander scale.

They cannot—well, they should not—spoon-feed the audience simplistic, meaningless junk. I compare movies to food. There are health food movies, and there are junk food movies.

Their work should not just sit there like a bag of chips. Of course, as I tell them, people like chips, and following that model, like junk food movies. One can earn a pretty solid living making junk food, but you cannot really live on junk food.

One way or another, all of my students want to make a living in the film industry. Making art and making a living can be tough desires to combine.

I read a screenplay recently, and I am getting paid to evaluate it. The script was in really bad shape, and I dreaded the idea of talking to the writer, telling him how much I didn't like it. While I knew that I couldn't tell him it sucks, I could point out what is wrong with it, what is right with it and what it needs in order to be a good movie. So, we finally spoke, he knows that it needs work and he was really receptive to my ideas for it. If I got hired to rewrite the screenplay, I would try to find something in this story, something I could work with, something that I could make entertaining and, if I am lucky, meaningful. I would do my best on the job and, if I do my best, it just might wind up being a pretty decent screenplay. So, why do I put myself through this? Why am I going to work so hard on it? Because this is what I want to do for a living.

I read screenplays all the time. I grade them for students, I evaluate them for competitions and I read them for filmmaker friends who come to me for advice. From time to time, someone I do not know reaches out to me and asks me to read a screenplay for them or to ask for suggestions on how to get into film production.

Recently, a stranger asked me to read a screenplay for a film that they want to make. The guy can write and the film would be really cool if he could make it. The project involves many locations (from city to beach, east coast to west coast), lots of characters, stunts and special effects. So, like many of the screenplays I read, the "if he could make it" factor is where a lot of beginning filmmakers struggle and I offered him the following advice:

"I came to screenwriting after film school and working on the crews of movies, music videos, infomercials etc. so, for better or worse, I write with production in mind. I want people to pick up my screenplays and say "I can make this film.""

The bottom-line with your screenplay is the bottom-line. As–is, I think it would be expensive and complicated to produce. Now someone else might read it and jump at the chance to take on this challenge. My orientation has been toward really simple, micro-budget films because, of course, they don't cost that much to make and they don't cost so much to make because they usually involve small casts and few locations.

Unless you have very deep pockets, have connections to investors or are really good at fundraising, the big trick to film-making from my perspective is coming up with a screenplay that you can actually make, that is not going to require a lot of set-ups in different places, complicated effects or stunts and a cast and crew of thousands, hundreds or even dozens.

With today's technology, anyone can make a film and plenty of people are trying to make films. I have seen plenty of people start films and not be able to finish them. I have seen some great films made with simple, inexpensive equipment, and I have seen a lot of really bad films. The point here is to know what you're doing as well as you can before you actually go out and try to do it.

"So my advice would be to do what you are doing, get out into your local film community, if you have one, meet people, offer to work on their films, make connections, get hands-on experience and build up a network of people who can help you with your stuff."

Just like Elvis inspired people to start making rock music and the Beatles, inspired by him, inspired scores of kids to form bands in their garages. Simply put. Just because you have guitars and drums, there is no guarantee that you will become the next Beatles.

Today, you do not even need instruments in the conventional sense, you can make music by clicking some buttons on your laptop or phone even but, because you can do it, does that automatically mean that it is going to be any good?

With today's technology, however, anyone can make a movie and, from my perspective, far too many people are making movies and, not that I am a math whiz by any stretch or into odds and probabilities, it just seems that the more movies that are out there, the more chances for more of these movies to be bad increases. Some people see the glass half full; I see a little crack in the glass where stuff is slowly leaking out.

I used to show the 2002 Sundance hit Pieces Of April to my students. I quite like this film, and I always show it to classes right before Thanksgiving because that is what, among other things, the film is about. It is my favorite Thanksgiving film. Pieces Of April is a low-budget indie-style film. I say "indie-style" because, even though it is, technically, an independent film, it is deliberately, maybe even self-consciously lo-fi. It does, however, boast a great (well-known) cast—Patricia Clarkson (in an Oscar-nominated performance), Oliver Platt and Katie Holmes and Derek Luke—at the top of their game and, most importantly, it is well-written and directed by Peter Hedges. I show it to illustrate the point that, if there is a good screenplay in place, it almost doesn't matter how the film is shot. So many people throw so much time and money up on the screen without truly understanding and respecting the importance of having a good screenplay.

There is a line in *Black Swan*, "Perfection is not just about control. It's also about letting go." While, of course, in the context of the film, the discussion is about ballet, I have always interpreted it as also applying to film in general and, to some degree, this film in particular. At that point in his career, Aronofsky might have been able to make a film for more than the $13,000,000 that *Black Swan* cost, but he chose to make a gritty, grainy, bumpy, choppy and, dare I say it, imperfect film—albeit one with state-of-the-art visual effects. Would a glossier, higher-end production have served the story well? Sure. Does the story suffer because of the lower-end production? Not at all. Is there a commentary about perfectionist filmmaking to be found in the subtext of the film? To me, yes.

I first heard about the film Putty Hill (2010) when IndieWire reported that there was an issue surrounding the distribution of the film because they had used a song by the Rolling Stones without clearing the rights. I thought to myself, "What kind of idiots take a copyrighted song by a well-known band, put it in their film without paying for the rights and expect to get it distributed?"

On day 1 or 2 of my screenwriting classes, I always tell my students to never specify copyrighted music in their screenplays but, the vast bulk of the time, doing so will add thousands of dollars to the budget of the film—and make the screenwriter look like an idiot.

So, I had to find out what this Putty Hill film was and what kind of losers would be so careless about the music. The film, it turns out, is a micro-budget indie about young people dealing with the aftermath of a tragic event. The film was shot on lower-end video in just a few days and largely improvised with a cast of non-professional actors.

At the time that I saw Putty Hill, I was working on my film Stomping Ground—which is about young people dealing with the aftermath of a tragic event and which was designed to be shot in a few days, without name talent for no money.

This, I had to see, was a film that raised so many red flags for me. How could it be any good?

I really liked it.

The film is shot on slightly lower-end cameras. It does not have a slick, pristine look technically, but there are some really well-composed shots and the final image has stayed with me. The story and execution are simple; the style, mood and atmosphere are rich. I could go on and on, but, the bottom-line, the takeaway, is that financial or technical shortcomings do not have to be a handicap. Filmmakers need to know what they have to work with and focus on crafting strong, cinematic narratives first and practical, technical execution that will serve the story shortly thereafter.

Once, one of my students asked me if I would read his senior thesis screenplay, one of the biggest projects of his college career and it really got me thinking. Here is my response:

> Did I like the screenplay? Basically on one level, yes. If this was a movie, I would enjoy it but I think I would enjoy it in the way that I enjoy a candy bar or pizza. It tastes really good going down but, in the end, I know that it is empty, pointless, worthless and, ultimately, bad for me.
>
> So, as a guy who likes trashy, junky B movies about hot girls and bad guys and stuff blowing up, I liked it.
>
> As a screenwriting teacher, I feel that it is my job to inspire art, to get students to aim higher than writing screenplays for movies that appeal to the lowest common denominator audience.
>
> Of course, there is something to be said for movies that appeal to that demographic because it encompasses the highest number of people and, of course, the biggest possible box office for your product.
>
> So, honestly, your screenplay feels like a lot of other movies by people of my generation and the generation after mine, are movies that are based on stuff we know from having seen lots of other movies, not stuff that is based on our observations of the world around us.

When Scorsese made Mean Streets (1973) he was really drawing from the stuff he saw happening in his neighborhood. In the early 1990s, when it seemed like the long strange trip of the Grateful Dead was starting to wind down, there was this proliferation of younger bands clearly inspired by them, sort of emulating that stuck-in-the-60s sound (and fashion sense) and they got lumped into a sub-genre known as Baby Dead. Similarly, when Rob Weiss made Amongst Friends (1993) and Troy Duffy made Boondock Saints (1999) and all of those other people who made films about young tough guys they all had this detached from reality element that felt Scorsese inspired, like it came from watching films rather than from watching real life and I feel the same thing about your screenplay.

The hardest that I can be on you is to say that I know that you can do better. Your screenplay, with its glorification of sex and violence feels rather juvenile to me, it's a fourteen year old boy's wet dream.

Look at your project and ask yourself if it is a four-star movie, if it is a Grade A screenplay.

If produced, does your screenplay have the potential to be Citizen Kane, The Godfather or some other movie that historically gets four stars?

So, the point here is to be realistic about our work.

If you look up what movies are playing in theaters in your area, you will see that there are maybe 50 different movies playing in town. Of those 50 films, maybe five got a four-star review and maybe five got a one-star review. What does that leave us with? A lot of two- and three-star movies, basically pretty average stuff. Most films are average, just okay but not great and also not terrible.

In the past over 25 years, I have been hired to write or doctor around 60 screenplays and honestly, I do not know if there is a four-star screenplay in the bunch.

I know structure and I know formatting and character development, and people consistently tell me that I write good dialogue; I know about plot points, act breaks and all of that stuff but that's only the beginning, lots of people know how to do that stuff and that is why there are so many two- and three-star movies.

Sometimes, I worry about being creative enough, smart enough or deep enough to write a four-star movie and there is no shame in that. The point is you can teach the nuts and bolts, but I don't know if I can teach you to be creative, deep or smart—that is called talent.

How did I get into the film business? Now that's a hard question because I hardly feel like I am in the film business. Yes, I did it, I have now done what thousands upon thousands of people are trying to do, I have sold a screenplay (did not get paid especially well), I have been hired to write or work on screenplays for other people—again, not very well paying, actually minimum wage or less and that is not an exaggeration.

So, my suggestion to people who want to get into film is to make films, either put your own stuff together—shorts or features—make them good enough to attract attention. So that means that you need to know how to write a proper screenplay and how to do all of the nuts and bolts technical production stuff or you can become a specialist. I am a screenwriter now, but at one point, I could take apart a camera and put it back together with my eyes closed. Not anymore. If I wasn't a writer, I'd be a gaffer.

Do it for love, because you love film, love working on films. You can work on making your own films or you can work on films for other people, just sniff around the local filmmaking scene if there is one where you live. You might (probably) work for free BUT you never know who the next big filmmaker will be, maybe you, maybe someone you meet.

Noam Kroll: the first piece of advice that I would give them before they start writing anything is take as long as you need to think about your idea and, uh, and make sure that that's the idea that you want to stick with, because so much of the success of your film is already determined before you even start writing the script. If you have a, a concept that is really strong, that you can describe to someone easily, that gets them interested, that gets you interested, and that you could see yourself working on for the next one to three years, um, then that's setting you off on the right foot and the right path. And

I think that where a lot of people, including myself have gone wrong in the past is, um, we want to just jump in right away. We have an idea that we think is pretty good, and we just jumped in with both feet and we just got started. And, um, that's good too, cause you don't want to spin your wheels forever and procrastinate, but you have to find a balance because if you don't really assess what you're doing creatively, if you don't really ask yourself the hard questions about whether or not this is something that you're really going to love in three years when you've been working on it everyday. And you know, you've seen the movie a thousand times then, uh, then you're not, uh, you're potentially going to run out of steam at some point, if you pick the wrong concept. So I think number one, the biggest advice is pick the right concept. Number two, which kind of goes hand in hand with that. And this is something I'm focusing on for my next film is take the advice where people see age old advice that people give you when you're writing a movie that you should find a way to kind of make it personal, make it the story that only you could tell it, maybe it's about your real life, but it doesn't have to be. Maybe it's just about a topic that you understand, or that you're interested in, in a way that others aren't, or that you have a point of view on that others don't. So find this story that only you could tell. Um, and, and that's something that, again, I'm very much being cognizant of moving forward on my future films. Um, and then when it comes time to actually write the film, my biggest advice is, uh, it's just write it. It's going to change a thousand times. You're going to, uh, it's going to, uh, not only when you produce it and edit it, it's going to change and become a totally different movie, but even just in the writing process, um, be prepared to do many rewrites and get feedback and change it. Um, but with that in mind, when you do have your concept, when you are confident in the idea of, um, jump in, you know, do your outline, whatever it is that you need to do to get started. But once you get started, just, just go and don't look back and until you're done with the script, you go and revise it and just keep, keep plowing through. And I think if you pick the right concept, you're that excited about it, you'll have the stamina to see that process through.

Martha Stephens offered:

> I think also really helpful as a way to approach writing something small, like if you have a friend that's talented or even a relative that you think could really be interesting on the screen, write something with them in mind. If you know someone who's a fireman, and you cast them as a fireman, it is probably going to have some authenticity, whereas you cast the fireman as a king of England.

Ry Russo-Young: I would say that, on my first movie, I certainly wrote a script. And I felt like in retrospect, the weakest parts of the movie were the script. And so, on the second movie, I threw it all out the window, and didn't write a script and sort of wrote in editing throughout the process and other people were credited; certainly the lead actress, Stella, with a writing credit, because some of the stuff that she said, and improv was just incredible, and way better than I could have ever written. And since then I co-wrote Nobody Walks with Lena Dunham, and I give her a lot of credit for the script being good. So yes, I don't think I mean, that was my first sort of hesitation in talking to you is that I don't really consider myself a screenwriter.

The thing that I say to younger filmmakers who, if you're not a writer, I think it's very, very daunting to make a movie. And this is kind of the Joe Swanberg model, like, you can also just shoot a couple of things, something that you find interesting, and see if it goes somewhere, because maybe it will, and that will give you more ideas to take it from there. But that's sort of what I mean by there's like a million different ways to make a movie. I basically just kept adding on over the course of the year. I would shoot something, I would edit it, I would write more, I would shoot it, I would edit it, I would apply for a grant, I would raise the money, I'd compile a bunch of scenes, and I'd shoot it. And it's because we were doing it chipping away at a nice block and a bunch of different methods that felt story applicable, but also taking advantage of all the things that you can take advantage of when you're small, and you're lean. I mean, I would meet somebody at a film festival, or literally meet somebody at a party and say, "Hey, you seem interesting. You want to be in this movie with me? Show up one day." Do you want to play a theater director? And they'd be like, "Well, I used to do theater" and I'd be like "Cool." Here's a text, can you be the theater director? And then I'd have the actor come in cold to the situation and have an audition, you know, or whatever it was?

DG: It's such an exciting way of making a film. When you were doing that, did you have any sense of, for example, how it's going to end? Or is it that you just shot and knew you'd put it together?

RRY: I just shot and put it together. I mean, it was like I was sort of writing it as I was going. But I was also writing it based on what I had so far. And I ended up with a really helpful person's suggestion and editor named John Walter, who had looked at a lot of the footage, he had an amazing idea that I shot that then sort of framed the whole story. I think it's liberating for people to understand that there's so many different kinds of ways to make a movie, and you have to find the way that really works for you and your skill set.

TOM QUINN: I'll be honest, I think something that a lot of low budget filmmakers don't do that I become more and more interested in— and even in the films I've done—is just research. I think there's the first piece, which is like starting with what you have. But there is another piece: really doing a deep dive on; whether it's a job or a hobby, or a defining characteristic, or whatever. I think of when I used to work with (writer-director) Eugene Martin, and the one film that we did, The Other America (2004) was in a women's shelter. It was really helpful for me to see 'You know, he did the research and the research fed back into the writing, and the characters and the setup.' But you can stretch what you already have, the part that you already have access to. But then there's this other piece, which is like, "Okay, what's around in my community or my world, but I don't have access to right now?" But there is a relationship I can build there. I mean, research is great, because you can sometimes find elements of the story that you didn't know about and it really can spin your story in a new way. And it also helps you when you're researching the community because you might be able to come up with some of those plot points and complicating factors. You know, it's not what you know, it's who you know, and I always try to tell students "Who do you get to know?" And I do believe that on a low budget, they're also the things that are around you that you can build relationships and invest in and it's going to pay off dividends.

DG: If some 22-year-old came up to you now and said, "Hey, I have $60,000 to make the film. Do you have any advice?" What would you say?

ROBERT GREENE: To me, it's thinking about the images. First, start with the images. A lot of people would say, "lean into the performances," meaning, find people who can execute that vision, and I think those two things go hand in hand. Great acting can get you farther than anything else. But I think it's the images. I think, without compelling images, acting can go away very quickly, and then it just looks like acting. Without compelling images. It's difficult to edit. As an editor, I think the screenwriting process should be thinking about "as long as we give our editor things to work with." So, you're thinking about how the cake is gonna taste while you're baking it and often, when you're baking a cake, that's not what you're supposed to do. But when you're writing at a lower budget, you should be thinking about the taste, and you should be thinking about how the table is going to be set. And you should be thinking about what the lighting is going to be like, when you invite the people in to come have the cake and think about that, and, in the end, have a holistic approach. That's the way you can make something for $60,000.

Martha Stephens said:

> You just can't sit around and wait for opportunities, you have to make them for yourself. I showed To The Stars (2019) last year to some kids at my school, NC School of the Arts, and when I told them that I graduated in 2006 and, here in 2019, I finally had made a movie for over a million dollars, their jaws

dropped. They're just like, "It took you fifteen years to get there?"

I had to learn the hard way that the screenplay serves as the foundation upon which the director builds his or her film. I have had screenplays radically reworked after leaving my hands, sometimes for better and sometimes for worse. Still, I feel like having something to start with, an idea that is organized and in some kind of coherent order, when making a film is critical. That something is usually a screenplay, the initial physical manifestation of the answer to the question "What is this film about?" or, more accurately, "What happens in this film?"

A screenplay is an instruction manual for a film.

Yes, "screenplay" can mean a formal script with every line written out and all of the scenes described, but it can also organize and document the ways and manner in which a filmmaker aims to capture everything needed to tell the story he or she wants to tell. Even in the second scenario described earlier, the filmmaker has an idea of what kind of film is being made, he or she is not just coming up with random ideas to shoot, turning on the camera and hoping for the best.

When a professional sports team takes the field, court, rink, diamond, etc., they do not just go out and hope for the best, they have a Game Plan, a sense of who they are opposing and how best to play against them. A screenplay is a game plan for a film.

If you are reading this book, chances are good that you are interested in making a film but concerned that you cannot afford to make a film. If you fit that description, chances are good that you have watched Mark Duplass' practically legendary 2015 keynote address at SXSW where, among other things, he discusses the conception of the feature that really put them on the map. "When Jay and I made The Puffy Chair (2005) we were very clear." We had my apartment in Brooklyn, and my wife Katie's apartment in Brooklyn. My street was really quiet and I knew we could shoot on that. I had a van because I was playing in bands. So I was like, "road movie—that's good for a van." There was a furniture store in Main that was going out of business, and we had like two identical chairs we could get for $300. I was like, "Great! I'll burn one of them and that will be our big stunt in the movie."

Work hard, have fun. Know what you want to do. Know what you are able to do.

# APPENDIX

Someone suggested that I include a list of the films mentioned in this book. I thought it was a good idea. Years ago, on the last day of a screenwriting course, a student raised her hand and announced that she had written down every film I mentioned in class over the course of 16 weeks: 175 different movies. Whoops, it looks like I only referred to about 150 movies or shows here.

1917 (2019), Directed by Sam Mendes, Written by Sam Mendes and Krysty Wilson-Cairns; available on Hulu

Alison (2009), Directed by Polly Schattel, Written by Polly Schattel and the Alison Cast; available on Amazon

Always Shine (2016), Directed by Sophia Takal, Written by Lawrence Michael Levine; available on Amazon

Amongst Friends (1993), Written and directed by Rob Weiss; available on Tubi

Another Earth (2011), Directed by Mike Cahill, Written by Mike Cahill and Brit Marling; available on Amazon, YouTube, Google Play, Vudu

Avatar (2009), Written and directed by James Cameron; available on Disney+, Amazon, YouTube, Google Play, Vudu

The Avengers (2012), Directed by Joss Whedon, Written by Joss Whedon and Zak Penn; available on Disney+, Amazon

Bad Ben (2016), Written and directed by Nigel Bach; available on Amazon

Bad Boys for Life (2020), Directed by Adil El Arbi, Bilall Fallah, Written by Peter Craig, Joe Carnahan and Chris Brenner; available on Hulu, Sling TV, Starz, Amazon Prime Video

Badder Ben (2017), Written and directed by Nigel Bach; available on Amazon

Bella Vista (2014), Written and directed by Vera Brunner-Sung; available on YouTube

Birdman (2014), Directed by Alejandro G. Inarritu, Written by Alejando G. Inarritu, Nicolas Giacobone, and Alexander Dinelaris; available on YouTube, Google Play Movies & TV, Apple TV

Black Swan (2010), Directed by Darren Aronofsky, Written by Mark Heyman, Andres Heinz and John J. McLaughlin; available on Amazon

The Blair Witch Project (1999), Written and directed by Daniel Myrick and Eduardo Sanchez; available on Hulu, Amazon Prime Video, YouTube, Apple TV, Sling TV, Philo, Google Play Movies, Vudu

BlaKKKlansman (2018), Directed by Spike Lee, Written by Charlie Wachtel, David Rabinowitz, Spike Lee and Kevin Willmot; available on Hulu, Sling TV, YouTube, Google Play Movies & TV

Blood Simple (1984), Written and directed by Joel Coen and Ethan Coen; available on HBO Max, Google Play Movies, Amazon Prime Video, YouTube, Vudu, Apple TV

Boondock Saints (1999), Written and directed by Troy Duffy; available on Tubi, Vudu, YouTube, Apple TV, Pluto TV, Amazon Prime Video, Google Play Movies

The Bourne Identity (2002), Directed by Doug Liman, Written by Tony Gilroy and William Blake Herron; available on Peacock, Google Play Movies, Vudu, YouTube, Apple TV, Amazon Prime Video

Breathless (1960), Directed by Jean-Luc Godard, Written by Francois Truffaut, Jean-Luc Godard and Claude Chabrol; available on Netflix

Captain Marvel (2019), Written and directed by Anna Boden, Ryan Fleck; available on Disney+, Google Play Movies, Vudu, YouTube, Apple TV, Amazon Prime Video

Casablanca (1942), Directed by Michael Curtiz, Written by Julius J. Epstein, Philip G. Epstein and Howard Koch; available on HBO Max, YouTube, Vudu, Amazon Prime Video, Apple TV

Christopher Robin (2018), Directed by Marc Forster, Written by Alex Ross Perry; available on Disney+, Google Play Movies, Vudu, YouTube, Apple TV, Amazon Prime Video

Citizen Kane (1941), Directed by Orson Wells, Written by Herman J. Mankiewicz and Orson Welles; available on HBO Max, YouTube, Apple TV, Amazon Prime Video, Google Play Movies, Vudu

Clerks (1994), Written and directed by Kevin Smith; available on HBO Max, Amazon Prime Video, Vudu

Colewell (2019), Written and directed by Tom Quinn; available on Hulu, sling TV, fuboTV, Amazon Prime Video

Coherence (2013), Directed by James Ward Byrkit, Written by James Ward Byrkit, and Alex Manugian; available on Tubi, Vudu, Hulu, fuboTV,

Philo, Google Play, Pluto TV, Crackle, Sling TV, Amazon Prime Video, YouTube, Apple TV

Creative Nonfiction (2009), Written and directed by Lena Dunham

Creep (2015), Directed by Patrick Brice, Written by Patrick Brice and Mark Duplass; available on Netflix, Google Play, Amazon Prime Video, YouTube, Vudu, Apple TV

Crescent Moon Clown (2018), Written and directed by Nigel Bach; available on Amazon Prime Video

Crimes and Misdemeanors (1989), Written and directed by Woody Allen; available on Amazon Prime Video

Cyst (2020), Written and directed by Tyler Russell, Written by Andy Silverman and Tyler Russell (release TBA)

Dance Party USA (2006), Written and directed by Aaron Katz; N/A

Darling (2015), Written and directed by Mickey Keating; available on Tubi, Pluto TV, Sling TV, Amazon Prime Video, Philo, Vudu

Dead Funny (1994), Directed by John Feldman, Written by John Feldman and Cindy Oswin; N/A

Deadpool (2016), Directed by Tim Miller, Written by Rhett Reese and Paul Warnick; available on Hulu, YouTube, Apple TV, Amazon Prime Video, Sling TV, Google Play Movies, Vudu

Django Unchained (2012), Written and directed by Quentin Tarantino; available on Hulu, Amazon Prime Video, YouTube, Google Play Movies, Sling TV, Vudu, Apple TV

Don't Go in the Woods (2010), Directed by Vincent D'Onofrio, Written by Sam Bisbee, Vincent D'Onofrio and Joe Vinciguerra; available on Amazon Prime Video

Double Indemnity (1944), Directed by Billy Wilder, Written by Billy Wilder, Raymond Chandler; available on YouTube TV, Apple TV, Amazon Prime Video, Google Play Movies, Vudu

Drinking Buddies (2013), Written and directed by Joe Swanberg; available on Sling TV, YouTube, Vudu, Amazon Prime Video, Google Play Movies, Apple TV

Elephant (2003), Written and directed by Gus Van Sant; available on YouTube, Google Play, Amazon Prime Video, Apple TV

El Mariachi (1992), Written and directed by Robert Rodriguez; available on Vudu, YouTube, Apple TV, Amazon Prime Video, Google Play Movies

The Eternals (2021), Directed by Chloe Zhao, Written by Kaz Firpo and Chloe Zhao

Faces (1968), Written and directed by John Cassavetes; available on Prime Video

Fort Tilden (2014), Directed by Sarah Violet-Bliss and Charles Rogers, Written by Sarah-Violet Bliss, Brian Lannin, and Charles Rogers;

available on Hulu, Amazon Prime Video, Google Play Movies, Vudu, HBO Max, YouTube, Apple TV

Frances Ferguson (2019), Directed by Bob Byington, Written by Bob Byington, Kaley Wheless and Scott King; available on Amazon Prime Video

Gabi on the Roof in July (2010), Directed by Lawrence Michael Levine, Written by Kate Kirtz and Lawrence Michael Levine; available on YouTube, Vudu, Google Play Movies, Apple TV

Girls (2012–2017), Written by Lena Dunham; available on Amazon Prime Video, Hulu, HBO

The Godfather (1972), Directed by Francis Ford Coppola, Written by Mario Puzo and Francis Ford Coppola; available on YouTube, Vudu, Apple TV, Google Play Movies, Amazon Prime Video

The Gold Rush (1925), Written and directed by Charlie Chaplin; available on Amazon

Green (2011), Written and directed by Sophia Takal; available on Amazon

Guy and Madeline on a Park Bench (2009), Written and directed by Damien Chazelle; available on Amazon Prime Video

Half Nelson (2006), Written and directed by Ryan Fleck and Anna Boden; available on Hulu, Amazon Prime Video, Google Play Movies, Vudu, Sling TV, YouTube, Apple TV

Halloween (1978), Written and directed by John Carpenter, Screenplay by Debra Hill; available on Prime Video, Roku, & Netflix

Her (2013), Written and directed by Spike Jonze; available on Amazon Prime Video

High Noon (1952), Directed by Fred Zinnemann, Written by Carl Foreman and John Cunningham; available on Pluto TV, YouTube, Vudu, Amazon Prime Video, Google Play Movies, Apple TV

Hollywood Chaos (2013), Directed by Abel Vang, Written by Angela Marie Hutchinson; available on Amazon Prime Video

The Hurt Locker (2008), Directed by Kathryn Bigelow, Written by Mark Boal; available on Peacock, Google Play Movies, Vudu, YouTube, Apple TV, Amazon Prime Video

In A Relationship (2018), Written and directed by Sam Boyd; available on Tubi, YouTube, Google Play, Vudu, Amazon Prime Video, Apple TV

The Interpreter (2005), Directed by Sydney Pollack, Written by Martin Stellman, Brian Ward, and Charles Randolph; available on Netflix, Google Play Movies, Vudu, YouTube, Apple TV, Amazon Prime Video

The Invitation (2015), Directed by Karyn Kusama, Written by Phil Hay and Matt Manfredi

It Comes at Night (2017), Written and directed by Trey Edward Shults; available on Netflix & Amazon Prime Video

It Follows (2014), Written and directed by David Robert Mitchell; available on Tubi, Amazon Prime Video, Google Play Movies, Vudu, Pluto TV, YouTube, Apple TV

Kate Plays Christine (2016), Written and directed by Robert Greene; available on Amazon Prime Video, Apple TV

The Kid (2019), Directed by Vincent D'Onofrio, Written by Vincent D'Onofrio and Andrew Lanham; available on Hulu, Sling TV, Amazon Prime Video, Philo, YouTube, Google Play Video

The King's Speech (2010), Directed by Tom Hooper, Written by David Seidler; available on Amazon Prime Video, Netflix

Jaws (1975), Directed by Steven Spielberg, Written by Peter Benchley and Carl Gottlieb; available on YouTube, Apple TV, Amazon Prime Video, Google Play Movies, Vudu

Joker (2019), Directed by Todd Phillips, Written by Todd Phillips; available on HBO Max, Hulu Premium, Amazon Prime Video, YouTube, Google Play Movie, Apple TV

Jurassic World (2015), Directed by Colin Trevorrow, Written by Rick Jaffa, Amanda Silver and Derek Connolly; available on YouTube

La La Land (2016), Written and directed by Damien Chazelle; available on Hulu, Google Play Movies, Vudu, YouTube, Apple TV, Amazon Prime Video

Law & Order (1990–2010), Created by Dick Wolf; available on Peacock, Sling TV, Philo, Google Play Movies, Vudu, YouTube TV, fuboTV, YouTube, Apple TV, Amazon Prime Video

Living In Oblivion (1995), Written and directed by Tom DiCillo; available on Hulu, YouTube, Amazon Prime Video, Apple TV

Love Life (2020), Created by Sam Boyd; available on HBO Max, and Amazon Prime Video

The Matrix (1999), Written and directed by Lana Wachowski and Lilly Wachowski; available on Peacock, Google Play Movies, Vudu, YouTube, Apple TV, Amazon Prime Video

Mean Streets (1973), Directed by Martin Scorsese, Written by Martin Scorsese and Mardik Martin; available on YouTube, Apple TV, Google Play Movies, Amazon Prime Video

Metropolitan (1990), Written and directed by Whit Stillman; available on Amazon Prime Video, HBO Max

Monsters (2010), Written and directed by Gareth Edwards; available on YouTube, Pluto TV, Crackle, Philo, Apple TV, Tubi, Vudu, Amazon Prime Video, Google Play Movies

My Dinner with Andre (1981), Directed by Louis Malle, Written by Wallace Shawn and Andre Gregory; available on HBO Max, Amazon Prime Video, Apple TV

The Myth of the American Sleepover (2010), Written and directed by David Robert Mitchell; available on Sling TV, YouTube, Apple TV, Amazon Prime Video, Google Play Movies

The New Year Parade (2008), Written and directed by Tom Quinn; N/A

Nobody Walks (2012), Directed by Ry-Russo Young, Written by Ry Russo-Young and Lena Dunham; available on Amazon Prime Video, Google Play Movies, YouTube, Vudu

Nomadland (2020), Written and directed by Chloe Zhao; available on Hulu, Apple TV, Google Play Movies, YouTube, Vudu, Amazon Prime Video

Non-Stop (2014), Directed by Jaume Collet-Serra, Written by John W. Richardson, Christopher Roach and Ryan Engle; available on Hulu, YouTube, Apple TV, Amazon Prime Video, TNT, Sling TV, Google Play Movies, Vudu, TBS

North By Northwest (1959), Directed by Alfred Hitchcock, Written by Ernest Lehman; available on HBO Max, YouTube, Google Play, Amazon, Apple TV and Vudu

Once (2007), Written and directed by John Carney; available on Hulu, Amazon Prime, YouTube, Apple TV, Vudu

Open Water (2003), Written and directed by Chris Kentis; available on Hulu, Apple TV, Amazon Prime Video, YouTube, Google Play, Vudu

Orphans (2007), Written and directed by Ry-Russo Young

The Other America (2004), Written and directed by Eugene Martin; available on Prime Video

Paranoid Park (2007), Written and directed by Gus Van Zant; available on Amazon Prime Video

Paranormal Activity (2007–2015), Written and directed by Oren Peli; available on Hulu, Starz, Philo, Google Play Movies, Apple TV, Sling TV, Amazon Prime Video, YouTube, Vudu

Pet Sematary (1989), Directed by Mary Lambert, Written by Stephen King; available on Hulu, Sling TV, Amazon Prime Video, Paramount+, Philo, Vudu

Pi (1998), Written and directed by Darren Aronofsky; available on Hulu, Amazon Prime Video, YouTube, Google Play, Apple TV, Vudu

Pieces Of April (2003), Written and directed by Peter Hodges; available on Hulu, fuboTV, Showtime, Google Play Movies, Vudu, Sling TV, Amazon Prime Video, YouTube, Apple TV, Showtime Anytime

Pirates of the Caribbean (2003), Directed by Gore Verbinski, Written by Ted Elliott and Terry Rossio; available on Disney+, YouTube, Google Play, Apple TV, Vudu, Amazon Prime Video

The Pity Card (2006), Directed by Bob Odenkirk, Written by Bob Odenkirk, Simon Hedberg and Derek Waters; sporadically available on

Primer (2004), Written and directed by Shane Carruth; available on YouTube, Amazon Prime Video, Google Play Movies, Apple TV

Psychosynthesis (2020), Directed by Noam Kroll; available on Amazon Prime Video

The Puffy Chair (2005), Written and directed by Jay and Mark Duplass; available on Amazon Prime Video

Putty Hill (2010), Directed by Matthew Porterfield, Written by Matthew Porterfield and Jordan Mintzer; available on Amazon Prime Video, Apple TV

Queen of Earth (2015), Written and directed by Alex Ross Perry; available on Sling TV, YouTube, Apple TV, Amazon Prime Video, Google Play Movies

Quiet City (2007), Written and directed by Aaron Katz and Erin Fisher

A Quiet Place (2018), Directed by John Krasinski, Written by Bryan Woods and Scott Beck; available on Hulu, YouTube, Google Play Movies, Apple TV, Sling TV, Vudu, Amazon Prime Video

Quiet River (2014), Directed by Polly Schattel, Written by Polly Schattel and Rae Becka; available on Prime Video

Rango (2011), Directed by Gore Verbinski, Written by John Logan; available on Netflix, Google Play Movies, Amazon Prime Video, YouTube, Vudu, Apple TV

Repulsion (1965), Directed Roman Polanski, Written by Roman Polanski and Gerard Bach; available on Vudu, YouTube, Apple TV, Amazon Prime Video, Google Play Movies

Reservoir Dogs (1992), Written and directed by Quentin Tarantino; available on YouTube, Amazon Prime Video, Apple TV, Google Play Movies, Vudu

The Return of the Secaucus Seven (1979), Written and directed by John Sayles; available on Sling TV, Apple TV, Amazon Prime Video

The Rider (2017), Written and directed by Chloe Zhao; available on Hulu, Starz, Philo, YouTube, Apple TV, Sling TV. Amazon Prime Video, Vudu, Google Play Movies

Rocky (1976), Directed by John G. Avildsen, Written by Sylvester Stallone; available on HBO Max, Amazon Prime Video, Google Play Movies, Vudu, Hulu, YouTube, Apple TV

Rope (1948), Directed by Alfred Hitchcock, Written by Hume Cronyn and Patrick Hamilton; available on YouTube, Apple TV, Amazon Prime Video, Google Play Movies, Vudu

Safety Not Guaranteed (2012), Directed by Colin Trevorrow, Written by Derek Connolly; Available on Vudu, Amazon Prime Video, YouTube

Saturday Night Fever (1977), Directed by John Badham, Written by Nik Cohn and Norman Wexler; available on Google Play Movies, Amazon Prime Video, YouTube

Saving Private Ryan (1998), Directed by Steven Spielberg, Written by Robert Rodat; available on Sling, fuboTV, Amazon Prime Video, Philo

School of Rock (2004), Directed by Richard Linklater, Written by Mike White; available on Amazon Prime Video, YouTube, Google Play Movies, Paramount+, Vudu, Apple TV

Seclusion (2022), Directed by Lovinder Gill, Written by Ross Mihalko, release date TBA

See The Sea (1997), Written and directed by Francois Ozon; available on YouTube

Shadows on the Road (2018), Directed by Noam Kroll, Written by Noam Kroll and Jennifer Stulberg; available on Tubi

Short Cuts (1993), Directed by Robert Altman, Written by Robert Altman and Frank Barhydt; N/A

Signs of Life (1989), Directed by John David Coles, Written by Mark Malone; available on Amazon Prime Video

Slacker (1990), Written and directed by Richard Linklater; available on Google Play

The Social Network (2010), Directed by David Fincher, Written by Aaron Sorkin; available on Hulu, Vudu, Amazon Prime Video

Songs My Brothers Taught Me (2015), Written and directed by Chloe Zhao; available on Amazon Prime Video, Vudu, YouTube, Google Play Movies & TV

South Park (1997), Created by Trey Parker, Matt Stone, Brian Graden; available on Hulu, HBO Max, Philo, Apple TV, Vudu, YouTube TV, FuboTV, YouTube, Google Play Movies, Amazon Prime Video

Spider (2007), Directed by Nash Edgerton, Written by Nash Edgerton and David Michod; available on Amazon Prime Video

Spotlight (2015), Directed by Tom McCarthy, Written by Tom McCarthy and Josh Singer; available on Netflix, Google Play Movies, Vudu, YouTube, Apple TV, Amazon Prime Video

Star Wars (1977), Written and directed by George Lucas; available on Google Play Movies & TV, Amazon Prime Video, Apple TV

To The Stars (2019), Directed by Martha Stephens, Written by Shannon Bradley-Colleary; available on Hulu, YouTube, Vudu, Amazon Prime Video, Google Play, Apple TV

The Station Agent (2003), Written and directed by Tom McCarthy; available on Google Play Movies & TV, Vudu, Amazon Prime Video

Steelmanville Road (2017), Written and directed by Nigel Bach; available on Amazon Prime Video

Stomping Ground (2016), Written and directed by David J. Greenberg; available on Prime Video

Sugar (2008), Written and directed by Anna Boden and Ryan Fleck; available on Hulu, Amazon Prime Video, Vudu, Google Play Movies, Starz, Philo, YouTube, Apple TV

Taken (2008), Directed by Pierre Morel, Written by Luc Besson and Robert Mark Kamen; available on Hulu, Starz, YouTube, Apple TV, Sling TV, Philo, Google Play Movies. Vudu

The Tenant (1976), Directed by Roman Polanski, Written by Roland Topor and Gerard Bach; available on YouTube, Google Play, Amazon Prime Video, Apple TV

The Terminator (1984), Written and directed by James Cameron and Gale Anne Hurd; available on YouTube, Google Play Movies, Vudu, Amazon Prime Video, Apple TV, YouTube TV

Territory (2005), Written and directed by Lawrence Michael Levine; N/A

Thunder Road {short} (2016), Written and directed by Jim Cummings; available on Amazon Prime, YouTube, Google Play, Apple TV

Thunder Road (2018), Written and directed by Jim Cummings; available on Amazon Prime Video, Google Play Movies, YouTube, Apple TV

Tiny Furniture (2010), Written and directed by Lena Dunham; available on Sling TV, YouTube, Amazon Prime Video, Google Play Movies

Tootsie (1982), Directed by Sydney Pollack, Written by Don McGuire and Larry Gelbart; available on Hulu, Starz, Philo, YouTube, Apple TV, Sling TV, Amazon Prime Video, Vudu, Google Play Movies

Touch Of Evil (1958), Written and directed by Orson Welles and Whit Masterson; available on YouTube, Apple TV, Amazon Prime Video, Google Play Movies, Vudu

The True Meaning of Cool (1995), Written and directed by David J. Greenberg; available on YouTube and Vimeo

Us (2019), Written and directed by Jordan Peele; available on YouTube, Vudu, Google Play Movies, Amazon Prime Video

Whiplash (2014), Written and directed by Damien Chazelle; available on Hulu, Starz, Philo, YouTube, Apple TV, Sling TV, Amazon Prime Video, Vudu, Google Play Movies

Wild Canaries (2014), Written and directed by Lawrence Levine; available on YouTube, Apple TV, Google Play Movies, Amazon Prime Video

The Witch (2015), Written and directed by Robert Eggers; available on Hulu, fuboTV, Showtime, Apple TV, Google Play Movies, Sling TV, Amazon Prime Video, Vudu, YouTube, Showtime Anytime

You Won't Miss Me (2009), Directed by Ry-Russo Young, Written by Ry-Russo Young and Stella Schnabel; available on Amazon Prime Video

Special thanks to Anna Greenberg for her extraordinary help with this appendix

# INDEX